Contemplative
WICCa

For Lucille and Michael

Contemplative
WICCa

Reflections on Contemplative
Practice for Pagans

TERESA
CHUPP

AE◈N

Published 2019 by

Aeon Books
12 New College Parade
Finchley Road
London
NW3 5EP

Copyright © 2019 by Teresa Chupp

British Library Cataloguing in Publication Data

A C.I.P. for this book is available from the British Library

ISBN-13: 978-1-91159-709-4

Cover and page design by Alexandra Thornton

www.aeonbooks.co.uk

About the Author

Teresa Chupp has practiced Wicca as a solitary and in various covens since 1989. She holds an MA in Theology from the Graduate Theological Union, and an MA in Psychology from the University of California, Riverside. She is a member of the American Academy of Religion and the National Coalition of Independent Scholars, and resides in northern California.

To learn more about her work, visit her blog, contemplativewicca.wordpress.com.

Contents

Foreword

Teresa Chupp has produced an immensely useful contribution both to Witchcraft and to Neopagan and Wiccan studies by constructing this insightful work that shapes foundation and contour, supporting the theological movement within Modern Paganism. A fulsome spirituality shines forth in these pages, one that embraces cosmology, spiritual life, and socially interconnected realities, and thus illuminates a certain path. Her goal is not to convince all Wiccans or Modern Pagans that a theological dimension is right for every adherent throughout the complex realm of currently practicing pagans. Rather, her interest lies in building a perspective and practice for those who do respond to the paradigm, and who wish to develop structures that facilitate enhanced cultural visibility and well-defined bases for inter-faith dialogue.

Selecting a doctrinally free, experience based, and widely recognized umbrella term—contemplative—as the housing for her project, Chupp enters into a very large tent of practice and meaning, one recognizable to most people, yet one that is owned by no tradition. She sees Contemplative Wicca as a contrast and complement to Traditional Wicca, and takes care to delineate what they share in common, and how Contemplative Wicca innovates in strategic ways. Her complements of science, monotheism, and contemplative practices, oriented to the Neopagan cycles and sacredness of nature, will make for an attractive option and path for many. Her well-described attributes of divinity emphasize a macrocosm-microcosm dynamic relationship between humanity and a holistic universe. However, it is a non-gendered essentiality anchored in Being that forms the core of her theology—a compelling construct that will strike a chord with a great many.

The chapter on 'Society' explores the social dimension of mystical experience, a category whose complexity and ambiguity Chupp helpfully unpacks. She critiques in a trenchant way the failure of social psychologists in relying on superficial understanding of the phenomenon being studied, and she presents mysticism studies under the framework of Evelyn Underhill's classic scaffolding as a more useful paradigm for exploring the inner life of Wiccans and laying firm groundwork for a Contemplative Wicca.

The excellent chapter on 'Ethics' anchors *Contemplative Wicca*. Chupp engages development theory as applied to religious and spiritual questing and examines the research on causal relationships between spiritual practice and moral and ethical development, finding that, in general, outcomes are best when the worldview of the practitioner is holistic and understands the interconnected dynamics of ontology (or, all being). She argues against a 'virtue ethics' approach in *Contemplative Wicca* and instead shapes a goal and vision that emphasizes effective harmonious relationships with oneself, others, and nature.

The chapter on 'Prayer' illustrates how one 'does' Contemplative Wicca. Her effective discussion on the types of prayer prepares the way for her teaching on 'Simple Prayer,' providing guidelines, instructions, and discussion on key elements of the spiritual practice of Contemplative Wicca.

In sum, Teresa Chupp has produced an exciting construction of Wiccan practice that intelligently, artfully, and strategically draws upon aspects of the human journey in the history of religions and in Neopaganism. *Contemplative Wicca* provides stimulating reading for connecting with vital elements of spirituality—one that is specifically Wiccan, yet innovative in theological theory and contemplative practice.

James F. Lawrence, D.Min., Ph.D.
New Religious Movements
Graduate Theological Union
Berkeley, California

Introduction

Traditional Wicca is usually considered by its practitioners to be a polytheistic religion of immanence that finds the divine in nature, celebrates the natural cycles, and includes the practice of magic. Similar to it, but with significant differences, Contemplative Wicca is an exclusively contemplative practice and theology of Wicca that is based on science, the concept of Oneness, and the traditional Wiccan veneration of nature. Contemplative practice both informs, and is supported by, this theology. Although there have been other similar integrations of nature and religious belief, this particular combination of tenets provides a unique and forward-thinking theological viewpoint upon which to base spiritual practice, and extends the current discussion of Wiccan practice and belief.

Today, with environmental disaster looming, it is imperative that we find a new way to live our lives, with new guiding values that will help us to heal the earth and each other. Because it is difficult to make sense of the world and society of today using the currently existing religious systems, many people have turned from mainstream religions, and are seeking spiritual meaning on their own. The extant religions are heavily encumbered with trappings from societies and worldviews long gone, and are not amenable to the radical alteration that is necessary to address our changed circumstances and the issues that arise from them. Science and exploration have changed our worldview considerably, and what is needed now is a new system of religious thought and practice, which will help us make meaning in our world, and live in it peacefully and sustainably. A contemplative, nature-based religion is especially well suited to address the issues we now face.

A Pagan theology would fulfill those requirements, but traditionally, very little formal theological thinking has been done by Pagans. This is primarily because there are innumerable groups and individuals with differing beliefs and practices and no central authority. Additionally, many Pagans are against formal dogmatizing, authority, and organization, seeing it as too restrictive. Nevertheless, in recent years, some have begun to construct Pagan theologies, and having a basic statement of belief and a clear definition of Wicca would go very far in establishing it as a real, legitimate religion to outsiders, as well as providing a better self-understanding for practitioners. If we can present ourselves unambiguously and with confidence, we are more likely to be given credibility by others. This same self-understanding can also enable us to better understand and appreciate other faith traditions, and cooperate with them in interfaith as well as academic settings.

Contemplative prayer is the core of many religions. This same contemplative core allows Contemplative Wicca to meet other faiths at their own cores, at the center of spiritual life, and to foster interreligious dialog. Time spent in meditation helps us to see and experience the Oneness that is so necessary to move spirituality into the future.

Oneness is the spiritual path of the future, and contemplative practice both provides the spiritual experience and supports the theological concept, guiding our behavior and our worldview. Monotheism is essential to this theology, because it provides the logical underpinning for the notion of the oneness of all things. If we can see God as the God of all that is, and can see that we are simply one family, along with all of creation, then the benefits of monotheism far outweigh any drawbacks. The monotheism I advocate is not strict monotheism; rather, it is panentheism, a unity where God is both immanent and transcendent: the ground of being.

> Today, however, the myths and creeds of popular religion have come under increasing (and deserved) attack, and many people have rightly left them behind. If religion is to survive for the benefit of mankind, and not for its destruction, reflective religious forms such as nonduality can no longer be confined to the elite (Michaelson, 2009, p. 97).

Wicca sees nature and humanity as sacred, and human society as collaborative rather than hierarchical. We are part of nature, and cannot be separated from it. Advances in science have enabled us to see the many ways that we are only one part of nature, not above or separate from it. Through contemplation, we can experience this, and can see the face of God more clearly.

Science can show us how God works in creation, and it provides the best support for the belief that we are all one. Pagans often see science and religion as complementary; and viewing science as a partner to theology can allow Pagans to see science and theology as united in one endeavor, rather than as separate and conflicting disciplines. This lack of conflict between science and religion makes Paganism well suited to forming a new system of religious thought and practice, which is so needed in our modern society. We need both science and religion. Science tells us what, how, and when, but religion tells us why. These two types of knowing are incomplete without each other.

Aggression has always been a part of Western society. Now that war and national expansion are no longer acceptable or necessary, but are, sadly, still common, we need to learn how to live more peacefully and share our prosperity. This can be accomplished by leaders heeding the ideas and advice of those who live in a contemplative manner and who can show all of us a new way to look at the world and each other, a way that involves thoughtfulness and cooperation rather than aggression. Although the contemplative way of life is not possible for everyone, its message can bring healing to our planet if we heed those who follow this quiet path, whatever their tradition. Today, there are many who no longer subscribe to the old spiritual traditions, and the theology proposed here could provide guidance for those who seek a new spiritual path.

This book is offered as an exploration of a new contemplative theology for Wiccans and other Pagans, as well as for those who may be seeking to incorporate contemplative ideas and meanings into the construction of their faith. In the following pages I shall explore what it means to pray and worship in this way, what kind of God inspires such prayer, what it means for daily life, and the importance of Oneness for our spiritual and physical lives.

NOTE: It is important to observe that, for the purposes of this book, meditation and contemplation are considered the same thing. When I use the term "mysticism," I include both ecstatic and contemplative prayer, and throughout this text I use the terms contemplation or contemplative, and mysticism or mystical, interchangeably, as mysticism includes contemplative practice. I do not consider magic to be a part of mysticism. For a full explanation of these terms, see Chapter Five.

Chapter One

Wicca

This chapter will discuss Pagan theology, as well as the importance for Pagans of doing theology at all, and outline the theology and practice of Contemplative Wicca, including its similarities and differences with other forms of Wicca. The main substance of the book will deal with the nature of God, ethics, magic, and prayer. There will be no discussion of specific rituals; rather, the ideas that support contemplative practice will be examined.

THE IMPORTANCE OF DOING THEOLOGY FOR WICCANS

Paganism has many and varied denominations, and none have a central authority. Practitioners are free to conduct an independent solitary practice, and many do. Beliefs and practices vary from group to group and individual to individual, and very little formal theological thinking has been done by anyone. This is why there is so little real Pagan theology: because there is nothing one can say that is meaningful, unless it is about individuals or small groups. Nevertheless, those small groups and individuals should formulate their theologies so that the religion will not remain so unformed and appear to have no identity or substance to outsiders (York, 2003, p. 157). In recent years, some have begun to construct Pagan theologies, and a seminary for Pagan clergy has been in operation since the 1990s. Pagans, however, cannot construct one theology that would apply to all Pagans. With the differences between denominations and individuals, what can be accomplished is coherent theologies that apply to individual groups and denominations, or a very general theology that would encompass all or most nature-based religions.

An attempt was made toward this goal in 1974 by the Council of American Witches, who drew up a statement of thirteen basic beliefs (Adler, 1986, p. 101). The Council disbanded shortly after this, and since then, there has been no similar group with the authority to alter this document. This is due primarily to the fierce independence endemic to Pagan groups, which prevents agreement on very much, and which causes distrust of large organizations of any kind. These two Pagan attributes are central to nearly all Pagans, but they also have the unfortunate effect of preventing larger unity or cohesion, even if it is in order to engage in beneficial activities, such as legal work to ensure religious freedom for Pagans. Although some, such as Circle Sanctuary and Covenant of the Goddess, do perform socially beneficial services, it is not common among Pagans. At this time, it seems there is no viable council or other group to perform this type of unifying work, so the original 1974 statement still stands. The statement can be viewed on a number of websites.

It is important to have theology guide our spiritual practice, so that what we believe, what we do, and how we pray do not contradict each other. With a clear theology to provide the foundation for ritual and other spiritual practices, those practices are more meaningful and satisfying because they are coherent, and are congruent with what you believe. Theology also provides an excellent base for one's ethical system. With a coherent theology, the ethical values and practices that flow from it can provide a satisfying, clear, and reliable guide for decisions and behavior, and for all of one's life.

Additionally, having a basic statement of belief and a clear definition of Wicca would go very far in establishing Paganism as a real, legitimate religion to outsiders, as well as provide a better self-understanding for practitioners. If we can present ourselves unambiguously and with confidence, we are more likely to be given credibility by others. This same self-understanding can also enable us to better understand and appreciate other faith traditions and cooperate with them in interfaith as well as academic settings. This greater clarity would also improve public understanding and acceptance of Wicca, and Paganism in general.

Learning about other faith traditions should also be part of theological study, and other faith traditions can provide great richness of thought and practice that can influence Wiccan thought and practice, to its benefit. Although many Pagans abjure the more traditional faiths, particularly Christianity, this is not necessary. It is important to remember that truth can be found in all faiths, and new insights and illuminating practices can be incorporated into a person's Wiccan practice, without losing any integrity. Indeed, there is nothing to fear from studying traditional faiths, and mining them for their gems of wisdom. By the same token, such breadth of knowledge and understanding can enable Wiccans to realize they do not have to accept all the standard Wiccan or Pagan ideas or practices, and to formulate their own.

SIMILARITIES WITH TRADITIONAL WICCA

There are two aspects of Contemplative Wicca that are most like other forms of Wicca. The first is that the religion is nature-based;

the second is the celebration of the Wheel of the Year, the cycle of nature. It is upon this foundation that Wiccan ethics can be based, as we will see later.

Nature

Wicca sees nature and humanity as sacred, and human society as collaborative rather than hierarchical. We are part of nature, and cannot be separated from it. We are part of all its cycles, including the food cycle. We take the lives of plants and animals in order to survive, and eventually we become food for some other organism, whether a large predator or tiny microbe, and complete the circle. All this should be done reverently, and eating should be seen as a sacrament, even as death is sacramentalized in nearly every religion. We are not above nature, and have no right to dispose of it profligately (Taylor, 2010, p. 20). This cycle of taking and giving life binds us to all of nature, and is cause for both humility and joy.

We are also bound to nature by the simple acts of breathing, drinking water, and walking on the earth. Many organisms have breathed the air since it developed, and it has been recycled through successive lives over countless years. The same has been done with the water and the earth, with elements breaking apart when an organism dies, and being used again as food to build new ones. Everything we do depends on the support of our environment. Advances in science have enabled us to see the many ways that we are only one part of nature, not above or separate from it. When we can experience this, it can help us to see the face of God more clearly.

I find science to be one of the best sources of theological thought and inspiration. When nature is approached with an understanding of how it works, it is even more awe-inspiring than when approached in ignorance. Science provides the best support for the belief that we are all one, and shows us how God works in creation. Fortunately, Pagans often find a great harmony between science and religion, and form theological ideas from this. This lack of conflict between science and religion allows Pagans to live happily and productively in both worlds, and foster human progress (Kraemer, 2012, p. 61). Viewing science as a partner to theology allows Pagans to see science and theology as united in one endeavor, rather than as separate, and usually conflicting, disciplines. It is this happy partnership between science and religion which makes Paganism so well suited to forming a new system of religious thought and practice that is so needed in our modern society.

Sabbats and Moons

Contemplative Wicca follows the wheel of the year as many other Pagan denominations do, with eight Sabbats and thirteen moons. The cycle of Sabbats celebrates the turning of the seasons, and the oneness of all creation. The celebration of these holidays, however, is contemplative, with minimal ritual and most of the time spent in meditation. This can be done as a solitary practice, or as a group engaging in a Zen-like group meditation. This is in contrast to traditional Wicca, where more ecstatic practice is used, and ritual is far more active, including drumming, dancing, music, and so forth. For those who are members of a coven, all Sabbats and moons can be celebrated together, however, it seems more fitting to celebrate at least the waning moon alone.

All contemplative circles can be commenced with a casting of the circle, and a reading or sharing of a thought for the group to use to focus their meditation. The rest of the time would be spent in silent meditation, and the circle would be opened at the end. Doing much more ritual than this would take away from the contemplative quality of the circle.

DIFFERENCES WITH TRADITIONAL WICCA
Goddess and God

One very central aspect of Paganism is shared by Contemplative Wicca, but with a difference. Contemplative Wicca uses the same goddess and god symbol set as in traditional Paganism, but the understanding of them sets Contemplative Wicca apart from standard polytheistic Paganisms. Contemplative Wicca is monotheistic, seeing God as One. Here, the goddess and god are seen as simply different aspects of God, not as separate gods themselves. These symbols are ritually useful in a nature-based religion, as they very aptly assist in the celebration of the earth and the seasons.

Most Pagans worship both a male and a female god, and many worship multiple gods. This makes sense, as people also need God to be accessible, understandable. If God is so completely other, then it is hard to imagine what It is at all, much less pray to It. It is much easier for people to anthropomorphize and refer to God as He or She, at least to some extent, especially in ritual or group prayer situations. In an embodied universe, God is manifested in the particular things all around us and in each of us; so, even though God is One, It looks like many (Michaelson, 2009, p. 4). Michaelson (2009, p. 62) even suggests that monotheism is incomplete unless it includes the many. Another way to think of the many aspects of God is to consider them representations of different people's experiences of God. There are as many experiences

6

of God as there are individuals, and each is valid. God is just as real when It appears to some as a woman as It is when it appears to others as an elephant-headed boy. Since God is ultimately ineffable, the multitude of representations of God actually helps us see that God is found everywhere and anywhere (Michaelson, 2009, p. 105). Michaelson (2009, p. 106) also points out that, since God is ineffable, it is equally wrong to either deny or ascribe an attribute to God. God is Its own category.

The important thing to remember is that referring to God as male or female is merely ritually expedient, and does not need to limit the single Godhead in people's minds. Monotheism is not just seeing the Godhead as a unification of the distinctions between various gods; there is only one God. When reflecting theologically, it is important to realize that God is One.

Monotheism and Panentheism

Contemplative Wicca has more differences than similarities with traditional Wicca, the two most important being the practice of contemplative rather than ecstatic prayer, and the belief in one God. Monotheism is essential to this theology because it provides the logical underpinning for the notion of the oneness of all things. "Polytheistic discourse had become meaningless because, among other things, it was too anthropomorphic and, more decisively, it reflected a fragmented rather than unified view of the cosmos. Only a uniquely one god can be uniquely god, let alone transcendent" (Werblowsky, 1985, p. 12). If God is divided into various smaller gods, how can we achieve unity? Monotheism can be feared as an excuse for authoritarianism and intolerance, and it has been used as such. However, if we can see God as the God of all that is, and can see that we are simply one family, along with all of creation, the benefits of monotheism far outweigh any drawbacks.

Animism is a popular theological position among Pagans, where the practitioner sees certain trees, mountains, springs, etc. as divine entities, each worthy of worship in its own right. This is perhaps the most fragmented form of polytheism, similar to the magical thinking of children at the preoperational stage of development (Fowler, 1981). Nevertheless, although animism views all things as divine, thereby promoting a greater valuing of nature, the concomitant lack of transcendent awareness promotes a focus on immediate phenomena, and can prevent a larger view of life. Such spiritual nearsightedness can prevent seeing the cosmos and all its inhabitants as one.

The same concerns apply to more formal polytheisms, such as Greek or Nordic. God is present in all things, and all things, including us, are made of the same stardust and partake of the same life. In an ultimate sense, we do not have separate lives, but are all part of the life of the cosmos. From the vantage point of Oneness, polytheism simply does not make sense.

Mantin (in Blain, Ezzy, & Harvey, 2004, p. 148) states that for many, "monotheism is the antithesis of Goddess spirituality" because it is seen as a model for a hierarchical power structure. Taylor (2010, p. 206) points out the "enduring conflict" between monotheism and polytheism, which is centered on monotheism's historical abuse of power and its habits of social and environmental oppression. Christ (1997, p. 111) is unable to see Paganism as monotheistic due to monotheism's history of goddess persecution. This, however, is not a necessary aspect of monotheism. What most Pagans object to is more likely the oppression, intolerance, and forcible conversion that were

8

practiced by Christian cultures, for example, rather than monotheism itself. If Pagans can separate monotheism from its historically associated results of hierarchy and persecution, perhaps there can be greater acceptance of monotheism in the Pagan community. Monotheism does not of necessity commit oppressive acts; rather, it provides a foundation for the Oneness and unity of all things. The sacred is everywhere, not only above, but below as well, and God is present both beyond and within all that is. As you can see, the monotheism I advocate is not strict monotheism; rather, it is a form of panentheism, a unity where God is both immanent in creation and transcendent as the ground of being. This will be discussed at greater length in the next chapter.

Monotheism, by promoting the unity of all people, provides a better survival strategy for us, while polytheism provides a platform for tribalism and divisiveness.

> Monotheism by inclusion, on the other hand, is a very different, in fact syncretistic process. Gods there are many, but when unifying tendencies assert themselves, for whatever social and cultural reasons, the gods begin to merge, with either one name being the real one (as in Apuleius), or all names being equal since none is ultimate. The Divine, whether personal or not, is so infinite and absolute that an infinite number of manifestations and hence an infinite number of names of the nameless are only to be expected. As soon as you move away from total mystical silence (known already to the ancient pagan philosophers, as Odo Casel has shown many decades ago in his dissertation *de philosophorum silentio mystico*) and from the concept of the Divine Nothing, to the sphere of speech and utterance, then names galore become inevitable. But their

justification resides precisely in the assumed underlying unity—a unity which may itself be beyond the very possibility of word and name. Some people believe in a transcendent unity of religions. Others proclaim the transcendent unity of names. Our age takes it for granted that polytheism is obsolete; that the only polytheism still possible is monistic sham-polytheism (I call it "sham" because in the multiplicity of its manifestations it is held to express an underlying unity); that the most acceptable and respectable form of polytheism is precisely that generated by a fundamentally atheist religion (MahSyâna), and that to talk about god is to use the singular in either the exclusive or the inclusive version (Werblowsky, 1985, p. 10).

The cosmos points to only one God because the universe is a cohesive whole with all parts coordinated together. If there were multiple gods, then there would be multiple purposes, and a level of conflict that, ultimately, would be incompatible with life. The fact that we are here, in a universe that is mostly harmonious, indicates the presence of a single guiding force that I choose to call God. Basing our religion on the earth alone is not enough. To be a God of the universe, God needs to be much bigger, in order to have ultimacy, and be worthy of worship.

Ethics

Wicca traditionally has not had a strong position on morality and ethics, and this needs to be rectified in order to have a cohesive set of principles to guide our lives as well as to present to outsiders. A good foundation for ethics is our view of nature and humans as being sacred, and of human society as being collaborative rather than hierarchical, as well as monotheism with its concomitant idea of the Oneness of all things.

Christ (1997, p. 119) points out that society's prevailing Darwinian view of nature as competitive arose at the same time that Europeans were colonizing the rest of the world and developing an industrial economy. It can now be seen that such thinking has brought about the current threat to our environment. This competitive view is deeply wrong, as we are best served by cooperating with nature.

Michaelson (2009, pp. 39, 214) suggests that a practice that unites body and mind could help to lead us away from further environmental damage, and eventually reverse our dire ecological situation. Because Paganism is an earth-centered religion, there is no other way for practitioners to live than ecologically. Christianity can teach its followers to be either lords of the earth or environmental stewards, but Paganism does not allow such leeway, and the faithful must follow the ecological path. For this reason it is a clearer and better path to wholeness and sustainability than religions with scriptures that can be misinterpreted. When we come to see the unity of all things, we cannot imagine causing environmental destruction; it would be unthinkable to destroy ourselves, our friends and families, our world. This view of ourselves and our planet needs to be brought forward if we are to avert catastrophe. We have the knowledge and means to change and improve our human and environmental situation; what we lack is the will. We do not have the will because we continue to labor under outmoded notions of what is important. If we can learn new values and adopt them in our lives, we can change the world. It is specifically in this area that religion can help us, by showing us how to find meaning in our lives and our world. The religion particularly suited to this task is Contemplative Wicca, with its thoughtful consideration of spiritual issues, veneration of nature, and promotion of a collaborative social structure. These ideas will be discussed further in Chapter Four.

Prayer: contemplative vs. ecstatic ritual

Contemplative Wicca is the practice of contemplative prayer and ritual using a Wiccan frame of reference. Ecstatic prayer and ritual is not used at all, which sets it apart from traditional Pagan and Wiccan practice. Wicca has a strong tradition of solitary practitioners, and it is this model of witchcraft that can provide a reference point for Pagan contemplative practice. Contemplative prayer involves silent, often solitary, attention to God. There is usually little or no ritual, and the purpose is to bring the devotee closer to God and allow them to hear God's quiet voice. This means that the usual rituals that include chanting, drumming, and dancing would be supplanted by silent prayer and meditation. Groups could practice Wicca in a contemplative manner by conducting rituals that are minimal, and delegating most of the time for silent prayer or meditation. The more usual activities of feasting and singing could be done afterward during fellowship. Solitaries have the liberty to honor Sabbaths and moons simply by meditating on the meaning of the festival, or by doing visualization work, for example.

Contemplative prayer is usually quiet and often solitary, while ecstatic practice involves some combination of singing, dancing, drumming, and a group of people. Both types of prayer can bring us close to God, but do so by different paths. Ecstatic prayer can induce a mystical experience through the devotee's physical efforts, while contemplative prayer is simply a still waiting for God to speak, which can take some time. Contemplative prayer is rigorous and difficult, while ecstatic practice can seem more like a party. Participation in ecstatic practice does not require deep thought or reflection, but contemplative practice does. The two different paths may also require different types of personalities in order to be practiced with greater success.

Those who are drawn to solitude and quiet are often also drawn to the spiritual life, and find contemplative prayer appealing; indeed, they sometimes feel compelled to follow this form of spirituality. For them, ecstatic practice is not attractive and may not even work. Although anyone can profitably undertake contemplative practice, it is more difficult for those who prefer the company of others and who are drawn toward action. For these people, contemplative prayer can be arduous or even irrelevant. Contemplative prayer is not easy for anyone, but those who are drawn to it often cannot let it go, and are able to persevere in spite of setbacks.

The people who are drawn to contemplative prayer are definitely in the minority. In Western society, most people are extroverts, preferring the company of others over solitude, and they have held most of the power in society because there are more of them and they are more aggressive (Aron, 1996). This has been to everyone's benefit as, in the past, people needed to explore the world and extroverts were brave enough to do it. War and other conflicts were common in the past, and extroverted leaders were able to defend the interests of their people and increase their influence and prosperity in the world. Now that war and national expansion are no longer acceptable or necessary, but sadly, still common, we need to learn how to live more peacefully and share our prosperity.

This can be accomplished by leaders heeding the ideas and advice of those who live in a contemplative manner and who can show us a new way to look at the world and each other, a way that involves thoughtfulness and cooperation rather than aggression. Although the contemplative way of life is not possible for everyone, its message can bring healing to our planet if we heed those who follow this quiet path, whatever their tradition. Contemplative Wicca offers such a quiet path for Wiccans that is every bit as valid as traditional ecstatic practice.

Many have been drawn to Pagan practice precisely for the opportunity it affords to engage in ecstatic prayer. For them, it was a joy to find a meaningful religion that did not involve sitting quietly in a stuffy church listening to interminable, dull sermons and cloying, simplistic songs. For the first time they could express their joy in God and be accepted. Why would they ever change their way of worship back to something even remotely like the way they had left? They don't need to. God is there for them, as It is for everyone. Besides, people may prefer one method of worship to another, but still avail themselves of other methods from time to time as the need arises. Once in a while it is helpful or appropriate to engage in a period of reflection and quiet prayer, or sing in a joyful group ritual, even if this is not the person's accustomed method used to find the sacred.

The core of most human religions is mystical experience. Most, if not all, religions have a meditative tradition, regardless of the types of rituals that they practice. This has implications for Contemplative Wicca in two ways. With its emphasis on meditation, Contemplative Wicca has little overt ritual as well as very little dogma, making it barely distinguishable from any other contemplative practice. The second is that Contemplative Wicca is a natural bridge to other faiths in its basis on meditation and its absence of ritual and dogma.

Because there is so little to compare, the first point prevents Contemplative Wicca from comparing itself to other religions too favorably, thereby precluding rivalry and animosity against the "other." Time spent in meditation helps us to see and experience that all is One. Additionally, this lack of ritual keeps group prayer experiences exceptionally unadorned, and the practitioners without the need to argue over superficialities. The minimal dogma also leaves little to argue over internally and little to defend to outsiders. This is not to say that theologians won't be able to find arguable points, and to carry on arguing as they have always done. Nevertheless, contemplative practice should lead us to the place where severe theological wrangling is irrelevant.

This same contemplative core allows Contemplative Wicca to meet other faiths at their own cores, at the center of spiritual life, and to foster interreligious dialog. The simplicity of belief allows the practitioner to approach others with sufficient openness to learn from them and find new avenues of spiritual growth, and to promote unity. Living at the contemplative core helps us to see that the purpose of religion is not to differentiate ourselves from others, but to see and experience our togetherness as children of the same God, and citizens of the same cosmos.

Magic

It is necessary to address the issue of magic and spells, as this is an integral aspect of Wicca, and part of many people's practice. It is part of Contemplative Wicca as well, but with important differences.

Magic and prayer are related, and use some of the same techniques. As with all else in Contemplative Wicca, magic must be guided by the concept of Oneness. When we see that we are one with the universe and with God, we can appreciate the fact that the seeking after individual power is neither appropriate nor even possible. It is fortunate that the attainment of magical skill is so rare and difficult, because when people think of magic, they think of just the superficial effects, and they are attracted to the power. They do not understand or accept that such power requires real work over an extended period of time in order to develop the necessary spiritual and moral base, as well as the mental and intellectual strength and experience.

The goal of magic is to gain control over objects and persons, while the goal of mysticism is to see God and attain union with It. Without a spiritual center, it is easy for magic to lack moral guidance and either become ineffective or too dangerous to wield. I propose an understanding of magic that would include a spiritual core, and whose purpose would be to align oneself with nature and natural phenomena. The practitioner would work within natural law to attain harmony, not seek to circumvent the laws of physics in order to create a sensation. My notion of magic is one of taking advantage of events and turning them, rather than performing feats of wonder and obvious power. It is possible to do this through visualization. By visualizing the desired end, the attention can be trained to look for things that may otherwise go unnoticed and unused, and turn them to advantage. This type of magic takes a great deal of time, and only works when one's object is in keeping with the normal order of nature. Clearly, this is a very mild sort of magic, and not at all spectacular like that wielded by storybook sorcerers. Many may not even consider it magic, but it is the spiritual way of magic.

CONCLUSION

It is important for Wiccans to practice theological thought and discourse in order to clearly form our own thinking and guide our lives, as well as to engage with other faiths in interreligious dialog. This practice can lead society to new ideas and ways of living that provide greater benefit than we are experiencing now from our dominant religions. Contemplative Wicca's distinctive differences in the Oneness of God and the universe, and exclusive use of contemplative practice are its most salutary attributes, as they provide the basis for seeing the unity of creation and each other. Coupled with this, the notion of the sacredness of nature gives the foundation for a system of ethics that, although difficult, could move us forward to a more harmonious society.

Although Contemplative Wicca diverges from traditional Pagan forms in important ways, its basis in the sacredness of nature and its use of the Wheel of the Year and Goddess and God imagery allow its adherents to follow the Wiccan path. Unfortunately, it is the very things that would assist Contemplative Wicca to connect with other monotheistic faiths in a positive way—the notion of Oneness and exclusively contemplative practice—that Wiccans would most take issue with.

Chapter Two

God

When discussing the nature of God, it is imperative for us to remember that our perceptions and understanding of God are limited, and anything we can say is necessarily partial and biased. Nonetheless, we must press forward in this work to clarify our own ideas and understanding, and to construct a foundation for a system of meaning to guide our lives. To this end, I advocate a monotheism that is panentheistic, rather than the polytheistic theology of Paganism, and this needs to be explained, and its value clarified. Theodicy, arguably the most difficult issue in theology, must also be addressed. Although there are few things that can be said about the nature of God that are not unacceptably limiting, it seems that, with restraint, we can speak meaningfully of a God that is both immanent and transcendent. I suggest we begin by investigating how we perceive and understand God.

GOD AS OUR REFLECTION

Does the need to attribute personal intention or causality give rise to the religious impulse? Did people create God to explain mysterious events they did not understand? It has been suggested that humans naturally think in terms of cause and effect, and when a cause for an event is not obvious, one is postulated. In this manner, people may have devised the idea of God in order to explain why things exist (d'Aquili & Newberg, 1999). Situations that are threatening, stressful and mysterious, such as medical problems, elicit attributions to God most frequently (Spilka & Schmidt, 1983; Wikstrom, 1987). Early humans, like all people, had a need to find meaning in events, and since their understanding was limited to their own personal experience and point of view, they may have attributed intention to natural events they did not understand, personified those events, and inferred God out of those events.

Although religions claim a transcendent source, they all have human construction, so claims to ultimate truth cannot be upheld very well. Nevertheless, many people believe they have the only way to the truth and to God, so with limited ability to empathize, and limited knowledge of others, they attempt to convert people to their way of thinking and living. They may use their religious beliefs to provide an excuse to exert power over others and even commit violence against others who may believe, or only seem to believe, differently. It often takes very little difference to incite sufficient fear and mistrust to bring about persecution and violence, such as that which occurred in Europe during the Inquisition and which is occurring now in several parts of the world. For people like this, God is very limited and life is very circumscribed. Those who do not conform are punished or ostracized so their beliefs and way of life can be stamped out. Fear is commonly at the heart of this sort of behavior, the fear that results when people are confronted with something that is too different and provides too great a challenge to their comfortable and accepted way of believing and living. When the idea of God is left in the hands of small people such as this, it ultimately loses power and betrays the needs of the people defending it. They are left with a limited God who cannot provide all the answers. It is then that they cling most tenaciously to blind faith, with their rigidity and fear increasing, and they resort to violence, since they have nothing else with which to defend against a threat that appears ultimate. This unfortunate theological limitation will bring us all to the brink of destruction, if not beyond, unless enough thoughtful people step in and turn the tide.

If so many people have a small image of God, how can it be changed? How can a larger, more nuanced image be grasped by those with limited interest or ability? As society has evolved, so has thought and world view. People have progressed over many millennia from simple technology and social organization to our current state of complex post-industrial society. This slow, natural process comes about through the leadership of those who can see further and understand more, whose ideas and techniques take hold in small increments over a long period of time. People tend to resist change as it is frightening and disruptive, but it will be adopted if it shows a genuine improvement over the past. At present, many people are beset with problems that prevent them from having the intellectual and emotional flexibility to entertain new modes of thought, much less to change their lives. Now, especially, they want a simple God who is on their side and will help them survive. Nevertheless, a deeper and more lasting peace can be had by those who are able and willing to take the plunge into a larger, less obviously comforting idea of God.

How is this to be accomplished? A thoughtful few must move ahead and make their voices heard. Now is the time for those who lead a contemplative life to speak their truth and point the way to a more tolerant, peaceful future.

People have, throughout history, devised innumerable notions

of God, and come into conflict over them. This conflict has aris-
en because of differences in perception and understanding, and
our inability to grasp the truth of another. It is our limitations
that bring about these difficulties. People's perceptions of God
are limited by their own abilities, experience, environment, and
health. If we have been taught to think of God as an old man
with a white beard, with expectations of us according to those de-
lineated in the Bible, then it is likely we shall perceive God solely
within those parameters, unless we have had persuasive experiences that lead us to hold different ideas. Whatever framework we
have for perceiving and understanding events and objects will limit our understanding of God to what fits within that framework.

To expand our perceptions, we can undertake two things: learning, and contemplation. Learning and study expand our knowledge of the world and ourselves, but contemplation expands our
understanding. Our ability to learn determines to a very great extent how we perceive God. If we are blessed with only a simple
intellect, then our knowledge of creation and of God will be simple, without depth or nuance. The greater intelligence a person
has, the greater their chance of having a deeper, more complex
idea of God that could include paradox and uncertainty.

It is through contemplation, however, that we can achieve understanding and wisdom. Contemplation gives us a broader vision that provides the ability to see the world as a whole, and to
see that it and all that is in it is sacred. Maxwell (2003, p. 259)
calls for an "integrated epistemology" that would involve uniting
the knowledge of science with the understanding of contemplative spirituality to produce a more holistic way of viewing the
world and our place in it. This integration of science and religion

promotes an ecological spirituality, stronger earth stewardship, and the notion that nature and all creation are sacred. It is from this vantage point that we must approach our perceptions of God.

If we can accomplish this union of scientific knowledge with spiritual understanding, we can enjoy an integrated spirituality. Contemplative prayer provides the same fundamental experience to all its practitioners in all faith paths because there is a universal spiritual core that transcends cultures and individuals, and which mystics access. An integrated spirituality builds on this universal core, while accepting and even embracing the various cultural expressions of it. It can do this because each disparate spiritual expression of the truth is seen as partial, and not absolute (Maxwell, 2003, p. 266).

Because God is ineffable, and all our descriptions of our experiences are merely metaphors for the ultimate reality we have experienced, we can only grasp at part of this ultimate reality. And since any of us can only formulate an incomplete notion of God, what is required is acceptance of all our partial ideas so they can be assembled into a more complete picture of the Ultimate (McFague, 1982, p. 193-4). We may all see God differently, but we all see some true portion of God, so this diversity is not a problem (Gross, 1999, p. 361), rather, the very richness of our human plurality is a gift (Gross, 1999, p. 364). It is important to point out again that learning is essential, as it is knowledge that combats bigotry. The more we know of other religions, the less fear and misunderstanding will cloud our interactions with others (Gross, 1999, p. 359). When we accept other ways of seeing God, we can learn from them.

THE INEFFABILITY OF GOD

In the Christian theological tradition, God is father. In many of our current reconstructed earth-centered traditions, God is mother. Both these traditions provide a limited view of the transcendent, immanent God. The male and female principles represent different spiritual and earthly powers, and Contemplative Wicca brings them back together after the exclusive patriarchy of the dominating Western religions. This unity of the male and female principles can create a worldview based on cooperation rather than on war and competition.

Most Pagans are polytheists, and prefer to have both a male and a female god, at least. Often, multiple gods and goddesses are acknowledged. This is meant to include diversity in the Godhead, but instead encourages tribalism and a small worldview. Animism is also widely embraced by Pagans, but this is an even more limited view. Panentheism is a better way to view the divinity of nature as it includes all creation, while animism acknowledges only individual, unrelated spiritual entities. If God is seen as the God of the cosmos, the one God of all creation, then that provides an excellent foundation for unity, and support for the belief in the interconnectedness of all life. God not only transcends being as we know it, but is the ground of all being.

If God is so completely other, and is the creator and sustainer of all life, how can something so limited and finite as gender be attributed to God? God surrounds and is within all, and the very creaturely attribute of gender is simply too small to apply in any meaningful way. Although the use of icons and other representations of divinity use human forms successfully, it must be remembered that whatever we may use to focus our prayer or meditation, such symbols do not represent the totality of God; they are only devotional aids.

Since God is both transcendent and immanent, there are few qualities that can be attributed to God that do not limit It. The essential ineffability of God renders it impossible to adequately describe God beyond saying that It is transcendent, immanent, the creator and sustainer, the ground of all being. Thinking of God as He or She is misleading, as well as inaccurate. What we need to consider is that God is Its own category, and nothing else can compare to It.

IMMANENCE AND TRANSCENDENCE

The practice of contemplative prayer does not require one particular view of God; throughout history, mystics have experienced God as either vast and unknowable, or as their beloved, intimately known. Still others have experienced God as both transcendent and immanent (Underhill, 1974, p. 344), and this is what I propose for Contemplative Wicca.

To discuss immanence and transcendence, it is helpful to clarify the difference between panentheism and standard Western monotheism. According to panentheism, God and the world are ontologically distinct, and God transcends the world, but God is also in the world. All things participate in God, Who infinitely transcends all. According to monotheism, God is transcendent and omnipotent, omniscient, and omnipresent, the eternal and immutable Creator. God is far more separate from the world, and the world is seen as less sacred. The difference, then, between panentheism and monotheism is that in monotheism God is transcendent only, while in panentheism God is both transcendent and immanent

(Cooper, 2006, p. 18). If we accept a panentheistic view, we can see that God surrounds and is within all, and is present everywhere. God, then, is right next to you, within you, unavoidable and immediately accessible.

Because each creature, every atom, participates in God's life, all existence is sacred. God is around and in everything, sustaining all that is, and God is worthy of worship; but all that is is not God or worthy of worship. Worshipping trees or animals is an error with a grain of truth, because we can worship the divinity in the tree or the animal as God is indeed there, but neither the tree nor the animal itself is God. People found this distinction difficult to make in ancient times, and usually did not make it, and worshipped trees and animals. We have progressed far enough today for educated people to be able to make this distinction, and experience the joy of seeing God in all creation. We can create sacred space anywhere by becoming aware of and acknowledging the divinity that resides in all things, and see God everywhere.

At the same time, however, God is transcendent, utterly different, far beyond anything we can comprehend. If God is to create and sustain all, then is it not necessary that God be vast, so large as to be incomprehensible? Because God surrounds and is within all, God participates in the entirety of creation, not just what one individual is aware of. How else could God create and support such diversity? Just on our own planet, there are so many different forms of life that no one with a mere human understanding could keep it all in balance. It is this universal scope that shows that God is transcendent, and transcendence makes God completely other, while immanence makes God immediately present to each individual at the same time. Pagans generally prefer God to be immanent only, but for me, that is too limiting. As Michaelson (2009, p. 53) points out:

> Perhaps the great innovation of monotheism is transcendence: that God is more than what is. But we have had thousands of years of this innovation, and its necessary counterpoint is immanence: that God is What Is.

Since both views convey truth, they should be reconciled (Underhill, 1974, p. 101).

This would also mean that God is not a personal God, who attends to the prayers and lives of individuals, but a vast, transcendent, and immanent God that is both everywhere and above all, creating and sustaining the universe in ways we may never understand. God is so entirely Other, sustaining all existence, not just human life, and it would require incredible hubris to believe that God considers each individual to any significant degree in the normal course of events.

The omnipresent God, immanent in all creation, would know all that is and all that occurs, as it occurs through Its agency. This does not mean that God is necessarily controlling or directing the unfolding of the universe. Although God as transcendent and immanent can be seen as omnipotent, it is still unclear whether God can and does intervene in the normal course of nature. Occasionally, it seems, there are times when events occur in such a way that it appears some great intelligence is guiding them. It is satisfying to imagine that God is omnipotent, and can do anything, even things outside the laws of physics. In the conception of God discussed so far, omnipotence is compatible and perhaps even essential, but is it demonstrable? It seems that there is too much chaos in the world to support a strong claim of divine omnipotence. Nevertheless, omnipotence seems to be one of the very few necessary attributes of God.

Some Pagans see the world as neutral, a complex natural system that supports all life, not just human life (Kraemer, 2012, p.104). Seeing the world in this way takes the specialness away from being human and shows us that all creation is holy. Our misfortunes are not personal; they are simply part of the unfolding of life. What implication does this have for our behavior? If God is transcendent and omnipresent, truly the God of all, then what does this mean for the exercise of power and authority? How can we presume that God could be on the side of one individual or group only? Are not collaboration, cooperation, and sharing what is called for? What is more fitting is to attempt to live in harmony with creation, not to exert control over it. This requires the understanding of creation provided by scientific inquiry, as well as a commitment to peaceful living and the exercise of rational thought. We should do this because it works, not because it is mandated by some arbitrary law laid down by an ancient God Who is too small for our world.

York (2003, p. 158) suggests that, in the view of most Pagans, humanity, nature, and the Divine interpenetrate and are interactive. Pagans tend to believe that if God is everywhere and in everything, if everything we see is infused with God, then how could we not interact with and indeed influence nature and the Divine, and vice versa. Some Pagans even believe that God, nature, and humans are equal (York, 2003, p. 162). We do interact with nature and the Divine, but within the normal course of nature. That God, nature, and humans are equal cannot be true if we accept our view of God as both transcendent and immanent, however. There are no real barriers for God between Itself, nature, and ourselves, but since God is transcendent and immanent, God is therefore essentially Other. Although through magic and prayer people can cause change in the world, this does not mean that we are equal to God. If we are to be honest with ourselves, the magic we can produce has quite a small effect compared to what we may like to do. It is important to remember that each of us is one point in the fabric of life, while God is the fabric of life itself.

GOOD AND EVIL

Good and evil cannot be predicated of God; these are human judgments that vary according to circumstances and social values. God is creator and sustainer of the universe, and our judgments of Its actions usually evaluate the benefit of those actions to us without considering the wider implications. What we consider good may cause evil somewhere else. Thinking back to the comments about transcendence and immanence, it is necessary to point out that the events we deem evil are perhaps simply beneath God's concern. Unfortunate events do not mean that God cannot manage them; they just have a part in creation that we do not value, or that do not fit in with our conception of what is right and good.

Pagans generally consider evil to be part of the natural cycle, and seek acceptance and the ability to live in balance with creation. Although this works with earthquakes and tidal waves, it may not with suffering caused by other humans seeking power. To live in balance and cause no harm, we must cultivate empathy, according to Harrow (in Lewis, 1996, pp. 20-22). Only by using empathy can we see whether what we do may cause harm to others, and the only way to achieve real transformation in society is to enable more people to use empathy to direct their behaviors.

Christianity and other religions taught love for one's neighbor for centuries, with little success. People and society were not sufficiently developed to fully appreciate this and live it out. Now we are better able to see and understand this, and our society has evolved to view human rights as important enough to enforce. The charitable and human rights work that is done is valued and lauded by all, and work is even done to improve social systems so human rights are not violated to begin with. This recent development is the fruit of centuries of teaching and preaching by various religions, and it is a great achievement, although very long in coming.

People have always longed to be favored of God, and it is a wonderful feeling to believe that God favors one's cause, or people, or person, but that belief is a fallacy. Throughout human history, people have claimed God's favor on their side in a war, and wrought terrible devastation and suffering on their opponents to achieve a victory that they held as proof of God's love. Does that mean that God does not love the vanquished? Are the vanquished lesser beings? God created them as well, and they have divine life even as the victors do; why does God allow them to suffer so? A personal God who loves each individual could not allow this to happen. It is primarily human anthropocentrism that has developed such an image of God, but this view has been shortsighted. It is difficult to take other points of view, so the ability to consider that others suffer and have the same rights as oneself has mostly eluded people throughout history. It has been easier, and far more pleasant, to envision a loving, personal God who answers our prayers, or to explain that the devotee was simply not worthy if the prayers were not answered in the way demanded. It is easy to excuse the occurrence of bad things by saying that the ways of God are inscrutable. This is true, but not quite in the ways people have considered them to be. People are part of creation as a whole, and God is concerned with the whole of creation.

Although sometimes it seems that God helps certain persons to succeed in their intentions, this is not usually the case. The wise thing to consider here is that those who succeed do so because they are in harmony with God and nature, not that they are special or selected by God for personal attention. This may appear to be the result, but it occurred because the person, either intentionally or subconsciously, fell in with the pattern of the universe and thereby succeeded. Achieving such an occasion of harmony once, however, may not guarantee future success.

What is God? It seems most people prefer God to be almighty as well as good, but I find little evidence to support this view. For me, God is the source of all life, both the good and the bad. I prefer God to be almighty, the creator and sustainer of all that is, the ground of all being. This means that God provides the gift of life to things like deadly microbes and the criminally insane, whether we like them or not. God supports all that lives, and all that lives participates in God's life. If God participates in all life, then how can God be purely good, when there are creatures and events that cause us such devastation? How does God allow great storms or earthquakes to kill so many people and animals? How does God allow such seemingly pointless suffering? Why is there war? Why is there death at all? If God were truly only good, then there would be a creation with only win-win situations for all creatures, but that is not the case. What works out as a success for one is sometimes a disaster for another because the success of the one depends on the failure of the other. Does that mean God likes the successful one better? Was the failed one created, with a consciousness and a network of relationships and all the other privileges of life, just to provide success for some other, some favored one of God? This would render God as capricious and unworthy of worship as an ancient god of Greece or Rome. If God is not purely good, then is God evil, or merely imperfect?

For me, neither applies. It seems that there are genuine mistakes in creation, such as Down Syndrome, where the genetic code is simply off enough to cause a person to have marked dysfunction. Babies born with anencephaly are another instance. How are these people meant to function? It seems to be another case of genetic muddling that is entirely unintentional but that leads to great difficulty, or even tragedy. There are examples of imperfection found in nature, such as animals born with two heads or five legs. If God were really all-powerful or all-caring, wouldn't such mishaps be impossible? Michaelson (2009, p. 98) suggests that God is in everything, even things that are considered evil. Perhaps one way to think of this is to think that God is not good and there is no evil. Life is simply random, and there is no need to explain God's purposes in allowing bad things to happen; they simply happen, and this must be accepted and dealt with.

It seems that God includes evil, or what we consider evil, in creation, and considering the frequency of this, it seems to be done on purpose. Why are some allowed to live lives of such terrible suffering? Does God really need to challenge people in such a way? I think a helpful way to look at this is to ask what it is we consider evil. Is evil absolute, or just the opinion of the person looking at the problem? I believe that it is the latter. We frame evil, as we frame God, according to our personal and cultural constructs, and although suffering is evaluated in nearly the same way over the world, particular instances are often evaluated differently by different persons. I think that God, being transcendent, does not differentiate good from evil. Creation simply is, and life in general is what is important, not the particular good or success of one organism or even one planet. For these reasons it is difficult to attribute goodness to God if God is to be almighty. Michaelson (2009, p. 74) suggests that "...the content of evil is the mistake of thinking that it exists."

Life is understood by comparing opposites; to know life we must also know death; to see light, we must see dark; and so forth. "Hence if Pure Being—the Good, Beautiful and True—is to reveal itself, it must do so by evoking and opposing its contrary..." (Underhill, 1974, p. 40). Mystics come to know the union of opposites where the Divine dwells, and can see life as a whole. This may be the purpose of what we consider evil—to enable us to see the evil so that we may know the good.

THE GROUND OF BEING

God is the ground of all being, the life force, the space between atoms, the source of their energy, that which has not yet been explained. Perhaps, someday, we shall have explanations for everything, but as of yet, there are still things we do not understand fully, and must simply accept. One of these is the basic force that sustains life and energy as we know it.

God is the source of all that is. God is the foundation of the universe, creating and sustaining all things both living and inanimate.

This is the primary function of God; that which makes It God, as nothing else can possibly have this function. All creation is an emanation of God, and God participates in the life of all creation. Without God, nothing would exist.

To illustrate this, let us remember that the basic building blocks of creation are atoms, which combine in various ways to make elements. Elements become minerals, gases, and liquids, and can combine to form living tissue. When a creature dies, its elements reorganize to become part of something else, such as another animal. God does not just exist as the life force, but as the creator of all, infusing life into inanimate matter, and returning living tissue to its elemental state. "Dead" matter also has energy in its chemical bonds, and God is present in this fundamental energy, which is found throughout the universe.

Michaelson (2009, p. 217-9) provides an alternate explanation of this. The universe is a vast expanse of matter and energy, space/time, of Being. We are part of this continuum of Being, manifestations of God, energy coalesced into matter, and have no existence whatsoever apart from this expanse of space/time. We are part of the One, manifestations of It, and so is everything else.

Perhaps it may be the case that God is not an entity, but rather an event. Another way of thinking of it is that God is a catalyst. God causes things to exist, causes life to come about, and keeps the life force moving in organisms and in the universe as a whole. God is what gives life and existence to all things, differentiating them one from another. Nevertheless, all things share that common divine force, that soul or spirit that comes from God.

Searching back toward first things, a child will keep asking, "But where did that come from?" until the adult either admits ignorance or chases the child away. Usually the point of ignorance is right about where God is. The awe this inspires has remained with us in spite of our technological advances. The enormity of reaching the place, even only in intellect, where we can go no further, makes us realize that we are just creatures, after all, and owe our existence to something that is likely worthy of worship. Awe of this nature is not available or important to many people nowadays, but contemplatives see and know it very well.

CONCLUSION

People have tended to create their ideas of God in their own image, and this practice has left us with ancient gods that do not help us address our current situation. If we are to move ahead, we must develop an integrated understanding that includes science as well as spiritual insight, accept multiple spiritual viewpoints, and remember that our notions of God are partial at best, so that we do not continue to labor in divisive small-mindedness.

Science has taken over most of the former function of religion, explaining much of how the world works, and the use of reason has supplanted the practice of superstition. This has enabled people to better see the weaknesses in the traditional notions of God. What is required now is a new idea of God that is not as simplistic as heretofore, and that accepts life as it is. God is simply God, the creator and sustainer of all that is, not our friend or father or brother.

For Pagans especially, it is important to remember that God is One, and that attributing gender to God is only limiting and divisive. If we are to avoid tribalism and a small worldview, it is important to keep anthropomorphic God-symbols as symbols only.

Contemplative experience shows us that God is not only transcendent, but also immanent; that God is everywhere and we participate in divine life. Not only human life; all life is sacred, as all creation is part of God. If we accept this view of God, then we must also accept that our behavior must fall in line with this, and that collaboration and sharing are what is required, rather than oppression and aggression.

Good and evil are human constructs that seem to have little bearing on God and creation. God seems to allow suffering in a way we cannot fathom, and its only value for us seems to be to enable us to learn through comparison to differentiate evil from good so that we may guide our behavior. God is this union of opposites, and it is the contemplative path that allows us to reconcile and embrace the paradox of divinity.

God is the ground of being, the source of all that is. God creates and sustains everything, and we are part of God; all is One. Although we are sustained by divine life, we are distinct manifestations of It, and have sufficient independence to see that God is Other, not only immanent but transcendent. God holds everything in existence, and inspires our awe.

It is this fundamental notion of the union of transcendence and immanence, good and evil, of God as the ground of all being that is the most defining characteristic of this theology. It is from this notion of God that all else must flow. All our thinking and ritual and daily behavior must be guided by this acceptance that God is everywhere and everything is holy.

Chapter Three

Society

I now would like to examine how the science of psychology can illuminate our exploration of Contemplative Wicca, and the significance of practicing Contemplative Wicca for ourselves and society. Although psychology has accomplished little in this area for a variety of reasons, there are some helpful studies to review and other sources of information regarding the mechanism of contemplative prayer.

PSYCHOLOGICAL ASPECTS OF CONTEMPLATIVE SPIRITUALITY

Social psychology has attempted to measure mystical experience for many years, but is hampered by operational misconceptions and a general misunderstanding of the phenomenon. In order to obtain accurate data, mystical experience is broken down into various aspects and measured, but because these scientists do not really understand what it is they are measuring, the various aspects of mysticism are incorrectly identified and their relative importance incorrectly assigned. For example, in a discussion of conceptual issues in the study of mysticism (Hood, et al., 2009), the authors point out the various usages among researchers of the terms "mystical," "numinous," "unity," and others. If their understandings of the terms differ, then surely they have also operationalized them differently. If different researchers are using these important terms differently, then how can the studies compare? If the researchers had a clearer understanding of what a mystical experience was, they could operationalize the concepts better and obtain more accurate and useful data. There are, in spite of this, many very useful psychological findings that can help illuminate our understanding of the contemplative experience.

Personality

What can personality psychology show us about contemplative life and prayer? Who are the people who choose this life and find this type of spiritual practice fulfilling? Unfortunately, there has been little study of such people, as they are inaccessible to most researchers, and it may also be the case that few researchers have interest in this subject. It may seem that to live a life of contemplation and solitude, one must have both the desire to do so and the ability to be alone. It may be that those who are too extraverted would not be able to tolerate the quiet and the internal demands on their psyches, as they require more external stimulation than is compatible with contemplative life. Researchers found in a recent study that most of their subjects were unable to enjoy a few minutes spent thinking alone about a subject of their own choosing. They found that those who were untrained in meditation techniques preferred to do even an aversive activity rather than simply sit alone and think. Unfortunately, personality was not measured or reported in this series of studies (Wilson, et al., 2014). In a study examining the relationship between mystical experiences, personality, and happiness, the researchers found there to be no relationship between them; personality did not predict whether the subjects had mystical experiences, and mystical experiences did not predict happiness. There was no difference in mystical experience between subjects with different personality types, and there was no difference in level of happiness between those who had had mystical experiences and those who had had none (Argyle & Hills, 2000).

Another researcher has found something different, however; she has found that there is a personality type that is more spiritual than most. These people have greater sensory-processing sensitivity, which means they respond more strongly to novel stimuli, and hesitate before engaging in something new. This same sensory-processing sensitivity also is found in animals, and is a survival adaptation, as it enables the animal to sense danger or find additional food more readily. This researcher refers to this segment of the human population as highly sensitive persons, or HSPs, and has also found that they tend to be more interested in spiritual practice and ideas due to deep processing of stimuli and ideas, and their greater sensitivity to all stimuli, especially to the numinous. These people are often considered shy or antisocial because they are easily overwhelmed by noise and crowds and bright lights, and need more time alone than most to maintain their equilibrium. HSPs tend to be more thoughtful, cautious, and quiet, and make up about 15-20% of the population; they may have traditionally served as priests and advisors in early societies. This researcher believes that high sensitivity may have a genetic component (Aron & Aron, 1997).

Another study (Saucier & Skrzypińska, 2006, p. 1258) suggests that religiosity may be heritable, and not just a result of environmental factors. In a careful study using a variety of personality measures, the authors found that one measurement of religiosity is inadequate, and that it is better to measure it using at least two different dimensions—traditional religiousness and subjective spirituality. These two dimensions are independent of each other, but both overlap substantially with personality. Because of this overlap, they may be aspects of personality, but even if they are not, "they appear to capture important dispositions of the individual, dispositions to which psychology has paid too little attention" (Saucier & Skrzypińska, 2006, p. 1288).

In spite of the clear contribution made by this study, it seemed that the researchers did not have an accurate conceptualization of mysticism, and tended to characterize the constructs of traditional and subjective religiousness using extremes, such as dogmatism for the traditionals and eccentricity for the subjectives, which may have altered the results obtained, completely bypassing any information regarding mystical spirituality in their sample. Based upon the evidence I have found it seems to me that there is indeed a personality type with stronger spiritual tendencies, and that personality trait, along with most other personality traits, is heritable.

Evelyn Underhill, in her seminal book on the history and phenomenology of mysticism, stated that there is a mystic type of personality. Although it must be remembered that she was not a psychologist, and her writing was based on a review of the historical record, her work nevertheless offers a great deal of insight into how mysticism has worked in the West, and so I include her work in our discussion. She said that those who search for the Ultimate, the mystics or contemplatives, are found in all cultures and times (Underhill, 1974, p. 3). Although this search is shared among contemplatives of many traditions, it is not necessarily an indication of common personality; rather, it may be the result of shared values. The last two studies mentioned above have different findings because they have looked at different aspects of personality, and measured them differently.

Development

This section discusses the phenomenon of spiritual development, both the stages of development as well as how we move from one stage to the next. Ken Wilber and James Fowler each proposed different developmental models for spiritual development, and when both models are used together, they provide a very helpful picture of spiritual growth. My structural-developmental model of faith development, based on the work of these two authors, will be used to partially illustrate how people move toward a contemplative life and what that life looks like (Chupp, 1985). For our purposes, the entire developmental schedule will not be presented here; rather, the discussion of this schedule will be limited to the stages relevant to mystical development. Next, the work of Evelyn Underhill, the noted scholar of mysticism, will provide greater detail specifically about the nature of the mystic's development and the mechanism of movement from one stage to the next.

Spiritual development usually only progresses to one of the average, or conventional, stages. Persons who have mystical experiences are able to move to higher levels of spiritual development, and mystical experiences can begin at the conventional level. Conventional spirituality begins at the earliest at the age of eleven or so, and can persist throughout life. For the person at this stage, it is important to conform to group norms and follow the leaders. Although abstract thought is available to people at this stage, there is little spiritual self-reflection or independent thought, and religious practice is usually limited to attending the public rituals of a normative religious group and saying simple personal prayers of an intercessory nature.

Independent spirituality can begin in the late teens, but usually occurs later, and sometimes not at all. At this level, the person forms their own ideas and values, and does not necessarily adhere to the values and customs of their group of origin. The move from conventional spirituality to independent spirituality is often caused by a crisis that exposes the limitations of conventional functioning, and can last for several years.

Integrative spirituality is not often achieved, and never until at least the age of thirty. Paradox, ambiguity, and a pluralistic viewpoint are embraced, and the body and mind become integrated. The final, unitive stage is almost never reached, and is not exclusive to mystics. It is in this stage that one fully realizes and experiences the unity of all creation with the Divine. Those who achieve it may have achieved it gradually, in small incremental experiences, or in larger, more dramatic ones. It is important to point out that integrative and unitive experiences are available to those at prior levels of development, but for brief periods of time. Those who have arrived at the level of unitive spirituality live at that place every day.

Evelyn Underhill wrote the influential book *Mysticism* over one hundred years ago, and it remains a key volume on this subject due to her keen insight and thorough treatment of the subject. The developmental model provided above applies to anyone regardless of their specific religion, set of beliefs, or spiritual practice. The developmental process Underhill proposed is specific to the mystical experience, and can be used in conjunction with the previous model to understand how ordinary people progress in their spiritual lives, and the differences in that progress for mystics. Although her work was based primarily on the lives and work of Christian mystics, her model is applicable to spiritual growth for Pagans as well.

Underhill proposes that mystics all differ from each other, so each one's experience and development is unique (Underhill 1974, p. 167). Nevertheless, she described five experiences most people have during their mystical development that are not true developmental stages, but events that commonly occur at varying intervals along the mystic path: awakening, purgation, illumination, dark night, and union (Underhill, 1974, p. 170). These experiences help to illustrate the passage from earlier developmental stages to later ones, but it must be understood that there is no strict order in which these events are experienced, and some events may not occur for some people at all. These events also can occur more than once, making the progress through them more of a spiral than a straight line.

1 – Awakening: This is usually an abrupt experience (Underhill, 1974, p. 176). A person experiencing awakening is usually in the conventional stage described in the previous model, and has a crisis of perception, realizing the shortcomings of their conventional worldview and functioning. For the mystic, however, this awakening is more profound. The awakening can be an experience of God as transcendent, or immanent (Underhill, 1974, p. 196), and the experience moves the person to change their lives. Most Pagans have had such an experience in finding Paganism. Few have been raised in a Pagan family, so for them to adopt Paganism involved severing ties with more conventional religions such as Christianity or Judaism. For most people, this is a crisis of faith, even if a happy one, and one that changes a person's life fundamentally.

2 – Purgation: Mystics of many traditions often seek and endure privation and suffering to purify themselves (Underhill, 1974, p.

200). Each mystic must purge that which separates them from God, and that varies from person to person (Underhill, 1974, p. 215), so even though ascetic practices differ, the purpose is the same. This would not need to happen if people realized that self-inflicted suffering is unnecessary, and that suffering that is given is much harder to bear than that which is sought and constructed oneself. When we see that God is not all-good, but simply God, then such purification is irrelevant.

It is far better to seek harmony in life and to use the suffering we are given to improve ourselves and our world to the best of our ability. Since we all have divine life within us, the way of purification for Pagans is more one of finding sacred space than of purgation. However it is done, we must clear away the externals before we can get to that deep place where God and human can meet (Underhill, 1974, p. 312). One of the most appealing things about Wicca is the absence of the guilt and suffering required in other religions; I do not believe in a God Who would require such misery. Pagans do not even have a doctrine of sin. Rather than an ascetic practice, Pagans could study and adhere to their spiritual discipline and strive to apply it to their daily lives. This purification or learning process would continue as one moves into more independent spirituality.

3 – Illumination:

To say that God is Infinite is to say that He may be apprehended and described in an infinity of ways. That Circle whose centre is everywhere and whose circumference is nowhere, may be approached from every angle with a certainty of being found. Mystical history, particularly that which deals with the Illuminative Way, is a demonstration of this fact (Underhill, 1974, p. 238).

Illumination can occur partially, or occur before or after purification; one does not have to be a mystic to achieve illuminating experiences, but illuminating experiences alone do not make a mystic. Most mystical literature describes illumination. The difference between Awakening and Illumination is that Awakening tends to occur only once, while Illumination can occur multiple times. For this reason it is not truly a developmental stage, but a phenomenon experienced by those on the mystical path. It can be had by anyone in the conventional, independent, or integrative stages, and provides the motivation to achieve the union they long for. Mystics usually realize that the Absolute is not achieved in Illumination, and move on. They want the Absolute and realize they must progress to the "vast and stormy sea of the Divine" (Underhill, 1974, p. 265). Underhill proposes three characteristics of illumination: 1) awareness of the presence of God, 2) heightened sense perceptions, and 3) increased energy that may include auditions, dialogues with God, visions, and automatic writings (Underhill, 1974, p. 241).

During Illumination, the mystic can have an experience of union with God, but it is only a foretaste of true union, which comes later. The difference is the individuality of the person remains intact during a temporary, illuminative experience of union (Underhill, 1974, p. 246), while an experience of true union with God involves a sense of merging with It. During Illumination, some can become selfish and simply remain in the ecstasy of the experience without doing any work for others (Underhill, 1974, p. 247). Underhill (1974, p. 172) believes the Christian mystic is distinguished from other mystics by the resulting impulse to actively serve the world. Not all mystics have this impulse, however, whether Christian or otherwise, and active service is not always practiced even by committed contemplatives. Hermits, who practice the most intense form of contemplative existence, have abandoned worldly life because they are compelled to seek God in this way, and their prayer is how they serve.

Underhill describes enhanced sense perception as seeing God in all things, or "Cosmic Consciousness" (Underhill, 1974, p. 255). Cosmic Consciousness engenders a harmony between the mystic and the rest of creation (Underhill, 1974, p. 258) and can give the mystic unusual power over animals (Underhill, 1974, p. 260). For Pagans, ecological awareness and values are the practical application of mystical illumination that reveals the presence of God everywhere, or Cosmic Consciousness. The reason we protect other species and habitats and try to conserve resources is that we see that they are part of God, too.

Increased energy resulting from Illumination can take the form of increased work in the service of others as well as in the experience of auditions, visions, automatic writings, and so forth. True auditions are heard when one is in deep meditation without conscious thought, but can also break in suddenly at any time. Underhill (1974, p. 275) considers auditions to be clear and unmistakable, but visions are suspect and must be considered carefully before accepting them as authentic (Underhill, 1974, p. 281). Visions can be tested for authenticity by checking whether they are life-enhancing to the subject. Do they give energy, charity, courage, and leave the subject better off? The closer visions and voices are to pure apprehension and the further they are from actual external hearing or seeing, the more likely they are to be genuine (Underhill, 1974, p. 283). Nevertheless, even mystics go astray, with their visions sometimes not being genuine but rather the overworking of imagination. They can't be right all the time (Underhill, 1974, p. 270-1). It must be remembered, though, that not all visions or other experiences are pleasant. Sometimes we are instructed to remedy a problem, and this can be distressing, especially until the required work is done. Visions and other such experiences must be examined carefully for truth before acting on them.

4 – Dark Night: The Dark Night occurs when the blissful experiences of Illumination cease. The devotee feels bereft, and deeply misses the guidance and certainty of the Illuminative experiences. They thirst for the light of God and feel as if they have suddenly been abandoned in a desert. This period of spiritual quiescence can last for years, and it is difficult to endure with faith intact. To my way of thinking, this experience, all unsought, is sufficient purification or test of faith for anybody, so that purgative experiences do not need to be actively pursued. I wish to emphasize again that it is not considered necessary in Wicca to suffer in order to get sanctity points with God. Rather, we must use correctly the suffering we naturally experience, and correctly interpret it to have it become beneficial. We must devote the entirety of our lives to prayer and God, and be willing to live outside the mainstream; this is the sacrifice involved. Mystics must empty their minds to find God (Underhill, 1974, p. 303), and because contemplation is the complete withdrawal of attention from the external world, it allows the mystic to apprehend the Ultimate directly (Underhill, 1974, p. 299). This sacrifice is the heart of the dark night; one must abandon striving toward self-advantage in order to attain the end goal of union with God (Underhill, 1974, p. 397).

O'Connor (2002) believes that the Dark Night actually may be the transition between developmental stages from the more concrete spirituality of asking for things to a more mature, abstract spirituality of union with God. The Dark Night is unsought spiritual suffering that occurs for some of us, and we need to understand that it is simply part of the journey and accept it as such. This does not mean we need to give ourselves up to it as some Christian mystics do; rather, we should learn from it what we need to learn, and use that knowledge to contribute to society, as well as enhance our own spirituality. Perhaps the purpose of the Dark Night is to bring us to the point where we can genuinely give up personal striving and work toward the achievement of Oneness for ourselves and others.

5 – Union: "Being, not doing, is the first aim of the mystic…" (Underhill, 1974, p. 380). The ecstasy of Union involves definitive contact with the Divine and results in spiritual certainty (Underhill, 1974, p. 367), causing the contemplative to be constantly aware of their union with God. It is at this stage that one functions in a state of union with the Divine every day. The ecstasy of union can be gradual and consciously cultivated through contemplation, or sudden and unwilled (Underhill, 1974, p. 375), so it is not always necessary to enter a trance or deep meditative state (Underhill, 1974, p. 366).

Mystics, prophets, clairvoyants, and all those who see further can be considered the "eyes of the race" (Underhill, 1974, p. 279); they run ahead on the spiritual path and come back to tell us where we are all going (Underhill, 1974, p. 450). The importance of contemplatives to humanity is to reach the pinnacle of human achievement and then serve as an example of this to the rest of humanity, to show them our ultimate goal (Underhill, 1974, p. 414). Transcendent life is latent in all people to varying degrees, so mysticism and contemplative prayer is for all.

> Every person, then, who awakens to consciousness of a Reality which transcends the normal world of sense—however small, weak, imperfect that consciousness may be—is put upon a road which follows at low levels the path which the mystic treads at high levels. The success with which he follows this way to freedom and full life will depend on the intensity of his love and will; his capacity for self-discipline, his steadfastness and courage. It will depend on the generosity and completeness of his outgoing passion for absolute beauty, absolute goodness, or absolute truth. But if he move at all, he will move through a series of states which are, in their own small way, analogous to those experienced by the greatest contemplative on his journey towards that union with God which is the term of the spirit's ascent towards its home (Underhill, 1974, p. 445).

Without regular contemplative practice, we cannot attain much as true mystics. By just allowing occasional "visions" to come, we end up with shoddy, undisciplined ideas and practices. Contemplation must be practiced with discipline (Underhill, 1974, p. 300-301). This discipline yields more than spiritual benefits. Nidich, et al. (2005) found that the practice of Transcendental Meditation (TM) over more than 10 years was associated with better cognitive and intellectual functioning, even controlling for college education. In a longitudinal study of TM and postconventional development, Chandler, Alexander, and Heaton (2005) point out that ego and moral development cease for most people after eighteen years of age. Since meditation connects one's consciousness with God or transcendent reality or ultimate reality, these researchers attempted to explore whether, if such a connection is prolonged with repeated meditation practice, it would promote higher consciousness development. The authors seemed to find that the practice of TM produced higher-level functioning in their treatment subjects than in controls, and suggest that meditation, specifically TM, should be widely taught in order to foster more advanced inner growth and achieve the higher reaches of human potential. They also point out that their and others' "research unambiguously supports the theoretical understanding that people of lower ego levels simply cannot comprehend—let alone fake—the reality of higher levels" of functioning (Chandler, et al., 2005, p. 112). Further, and better, studies should be done.

Although the theoretical underpinning and methodology of this study is weak, their suggestion to teach meditation in colleges in order to advance human consciousness and ego development is intriguing, and likely a very good one. Is it possible, however, for all people to advance to transcendent or postconventional levels? Not everyone can achieve abstract thought, and not all people have above average intelligence, so perhaps not all people can achieve these levels of ego and moral development. Although everyone can benefit from this practice, how much would less capable people benefit?

As it happens, someone has considered the benefits of meditation and been teaching it in schools. According to an article in the

Huffington Post (Kaleem, 2015), meditation is now part of the curriculum in some middle and high schools. It seems that teaching students to meditate has been done in a few places for about 25 years, but has expanded in the last few years to about 18 schools in the US. With parental permission, students in the schools with a "Quiet Time" program can meditate; the other students simply sit quietly for the few minutes allotted to the practice. The type of meditation taught is Transcendental Meditation, which is not very difficult to do, so is approachable for the kids. Instituting meditation periods in school has improved grades and reduced violence. It appears that meditation has clear benefits for anyone who practices it.

Through this small effort, these children will grow up with a capacity for and understanding of meditation and will reap the benefits of this type of activity, even if it is secular for them. The awareness they will have achieved will bring them closer to seeing the world with a broader vision and greater empathy, and eventually change the world for the better. It is heartening to see that such work is being done, rather than leaving that development all to chance.

Mysticism and Psychopathology

Contemplatives have been considered suspect in the West. Those who meditate have often been seen as crazy or odd, and were shunned. Although this prejudice is declining and many more are meditating now than fifty years ago, many people cannot differentiate between a mystical experience and a psychotic one. It is important to clear up some of the confusion around mental health and mysticism. Mystical experiences can be positive or negative, uplifting and joyful, or frightening and disturbing. Although it would seem that healthy and well-adjusted people would only have positive mystical experiences, and that the mentally ill would only have distressing mystical experiences, one study showed that positive mysticism is unrelated to psychopathology. In their sample, "Positive mystical experiences occur as frequently among those who are psychologically stable as among those who tend to be distraught and troubled" (Spanos & Moretti, 1988).

> The convergence of hysteria, hysterical personality and asceticism/mysticism has been enormously exaggerated and exploited to the detriment of sincere religious commitment, serving little purpose other than disparaging a group (both men and women) whose vision of what is valuable in life and worth struggling for differed radically from a materialistic and secular viewpoint (Kroll, et al., 2002, p. 92).

Both contemplative life and Wicca carry stigma in conventional Western society. Spiritual people, as well as artists, can be prophetic, and so are frightening to others, who often reject them. The silence of the contemplative "speaks, implying a secret knowledge that makes people profoundly uneasy" (Fredette & Fredette, 2008, p. 208). Contemplatives seek direct contact with the Holy, and when this is made, the seeker is scarred for life (p. 227, op cit.). Once so scarred, the seeker cannot lead a normal life. Wicca is not a mainstream religion, and many still consider witchcraft something to fear and eradicate. Practitioners of Contemplative Wicca, then, can be marginalized twice over. "Being different is never safe" (p. 211, op cit.).

Although we might like to think that spiritual people are more enlightened and mentally more robust than secular people, there are instances where poor mental health and spirituality do converge.

This does not mean, however, that the mystical experience of the afflicted person is inauthentic. The mystic is not required to demonstrate fitness before being vouchsafed a spiritual experience. Mystical experience brings the practitioner into direct, unmediated contact with the Divine. Although these are intimate personal experiences, the person lives in society, in most cases. When a society does not understand or does not value these experiences, the practitioner may be misdiagnosed with some psychopathology. However, even if the practitioner has some real pathology, there may also be a true mystical experience present that could be integrated positively into the practitioner's life, and the life of the community as a whole, if that society were able to accept transcendent reality and mystical experience (Cook, 2004, p.160).

The problem may be more with those around the mystic who are trying to provide care, or perhaps merely passing judgment, rather than with the mystic him/herself. When society devalues the mystical experience or the mystic themselves, the mystic is marginalized, and the society is prevented from dealing with that transcendent reality that they consider so unworthy (Cook, 2004, p. 154). This is impoverishing for all.

The cause of misunderstanding and outright rejection is that the values held by conventional Western society and those held by contemplatives diverge too greatly to admit of sufficient understanding to allow an untroubled coexistence between them. When transcendent reality is considered using practical notions of things, most religious persons will be considered to suffer with some psychopathology (Kroll, et al., 2002, p. 94).

> Just as mystical experience is valuable and life enhancing to the individual, it has an indirect benefit to the wider community.

Where this is denied, and where psychiatry colludes in pathologizing such experiences, the whole community is the poorer as a result. Where its value is recognized and affirmed, it offers vicarious inspiration which is available to many (Cook, 2004, p.160).

It is when the mystic shares the community's accepted creed that the mutual understanding of the mystic and the community can most easily bring about spiritual enhancement for everyone.

Further studies help to illustrate this. One author found that "mystical experiences in the absence of a mystical interpretive framework often detract from subjective well-being" (Schwenka, 2000, p. 268). In another study, using American and Iranian subjects, Hood, et al., (2001, p. 703) found that there was a positive association between a religious interpretation of mystical experiences and mental health only in the Iranian sample. From this they inferred that if a subject lived in a more explicitly religious culture, religious interpretations of mystical experiences would be more likely, and such experiences would not carry the stigma they do in a more secular society. The crucial element, then, is having a socially accepted understanding of the mystical experience, and a way of deriving ultimate meaning from it.

Can the science of psychology help us understand the real situation with mystical practice and mental health? Unfortunately, it does not seem so, as the following examples discussed by Hood, et al. (2009) illustrate. Approximately one-third of the normal population has had some sort of mystical or spiritual experience, and importantly, those people also tend to enjoy psychological health rather than pathology. A different study indicated that self-esteem is correlated with deeply held conventional religious beliefs, but not with independent, unconventional spirituality. However, another study indicated that those who had mystical experiences outside of a traditional religious setting were actually more open and tolerant of a greater breadth of experience than those within a conventional religious tradition. It may be that those who are able to go out on a limb with their faith are also able to perceive and accept the uncertainties of life, including their own limitations. In a different paper, Hood, et al., (2001, p. 703) came to a sad conclusion: "The present study, therefore, provided a cross-cultural confirmation for the conclusion that mystical experience can predict psychological dysfunction, and these data supported a further, more specific hypothesis that such effects are attributable to the introvertive experience". In a 1993 study (Stifler, et al.), the researchers found that the Hood Mysticism scale, a well-documented and often-used survey instrument, was unable to differentiate between psychotics and contemplatives. It is hard to gauge the truth when studies find such divergent results.

The spiritual life is not easy, however, and contemplative prayer is not undertaken for purposes of relaxation or health. Contemplative prayer is spiritual work, and although it can be rewarded with ecstatic or illuminative experiences, most often it is simply hard work. It is hard work because it is not always fruitful and not all spiritual experiences are pleasant. Meditation can unleash unconscious forces that an unprepared person may not be able to handle without help (Michalon, 2001). Nevertheless, the more adept a practitioner is, the better able s/he is to take advantage of what others would consider regressive or disruptive experiences. Consistent work enables the practitioner to become increasingly open to whatever God wishes to provide, and to understand it (Hood, et al., 2009).

SOCIAL ASPECTS OF CONTEMPLATIVE SPIRITUALITY

How does Western society view contemplative religion, and what effect does it have on the practitioner? It seems that, for the most part, the contemplative life is a lonely road, especially in America, even though religion is an accepted part of life. Here, I would like to examine why mystics in Western society are so misunderstood.

The practice of religion has been supported by societies throughout the ages because it promotes enhanced moral sensibilities, internal freedom, self-control, insight, empathy, compassion, generativity, and prosocial behavior in general (McNamara, 2002). Religion has been the traditional method of promoting this type of development toward maturity, but has never been the only method. Today there are other methods of mental and moral development available to people that are likely more reliable, if less traditional. It is religion, however, that provides the foundation for the meaning that underpins everything else; religion tells people why. Organized religion has a mystical or contemplative core; and mysticism usually is informed by organized religion, but it does not need to be. Mystics often fit into an accepted creed, but whether they do or not, if they are unable to explain what they have experienced, they can be seen as mad or heretical (Underhill, 1974, pp. 95 & 104). This is more likely when they have no religious language to use and no religious community to address who would understand. Their extreme difference alienates them from society. Even when they have a shared religious language, mystical experience often is

so far removed from conventional experience that the same aliena-
tion occurs.

Often those who have valid mystical experiences are very unconventional, and may be rejected by mainstream society and even
considered mad. Their strangeness or unconventionality does not
diminish the truth of their experiences, because any vessel can
carry the light of God. The mystic Jacob Boehme is one example
of the drawbacks of such unconventionality. He was unable to describe his spiritual experiences so they were intelligible to others,
and Underhill (1974, p. 257) says of him "The very strangeness
of the phrasing, the unexpected harmonies and dissonances which
worry polite and well-regulated minds, are earnests of the Spirit of
Life crying out for expression from within".

Meditation and contemplative prayer may be a more appealing
path for those who are willing to forgo the comfort of social approval and forge ahead into new territories that may not be acceptable or desirable to the majority. This may be because meditation
is more appealing for those who engage in independent thinking,
while those who are more conventional prefer intercessory prayer
(Kaldor, et al., 2002). Solitaries and contemplatives have always
lived at the edge of Western society, even when Europe was experiencing its very religious Middle Ages. At best, it seems, they are
accepted as marginal members of society, while at worst, they are
not accepted and are marginalized even further, as they are today.
Theoretically, mystical experience is possible for everyone, and as
many as a third or more of survey respondents have admitted to
having had mystical experiences (Cook, 2004). Nevertheless, it is
actively sought by only a few, and most people find descriptions
of mystical experiences difficult to understand. Mystics are heroic

adventurers seeking the Divine (Underhill, 1974, p. 34). They have developed their spiritual consciousness while most people have not, and for this reason their pioneering is important to humanity; they are the only ones who can show us these things. This offers a vicarious benefit to others as it informs and inspires their understanding of their own experience of human life. Mystics have the strength and tolerance for unpleasant truths that allows them to dwell every day at the barrier that separates us from the transcendent. Because contemplatives live at and can see through this barrier, they can also point the way to the transcendent for others. Their lives of continual prayer and silent waiting enable them to become aware of the Holy when It arrives.

Historically, mystics often have had health problems, but as often have been long-lived and very vital despite their ill health due to the revitalizing effects of their contemplative practice and contact with the Divine (Underhill, 1974, p. 59). May it not be the case that good health is part of being average? Perhaps health and safety are enjoyed when a person does not take chances or does not do unusual things. Perhaps those who do new and interesting and important things, rather than just being financially successful and revered by society, are on the edge of society and do not participate very much in the life lived by average persons; instead they move into uncharted areas, eventually allowing the rest of humanity to follow. The price they pay for this is often very high.

> Now and then an artist is born, terribly articulate, foolishly truthful, who insists on 'speaking as he saw.' Then other men, lapped warmly in their artificial universe, agree that he is mad: or, at the very best, an 'extraordinarily imaginative fellow' (Underhill, 1974, p. 10).

By engaging in contemplative life, the contemplative opposes social evil by not participating in it. In this way, the contemplative functions as a social prophet and points the way to a better life, and does not contribute to the prevailing evil (Plank, 2002). We all know, however, the fate of many prophets.

CONCLUSION

Psychology provides little assistance in understanding spirituality in any of its forms, primarily because the researchers understand very little of what it is they are trying to measure, so when they measure it, it is improperly operationalized. Studies come to varying conclusions, and there are no agreed-upon definitions to guide research in the psychology of religion. Although there are a few clear, insightful studies, I agree with Hood, et al. (2009) that what is needed most in the psychology of religion is better theory.

The only psychologists who support spiritual striving tend to be clinical psychologists of the Transpersonal school, and of course, followers of Carl Jung. It would seem that empiricists could avail themselves of these writings if they wished to find theory that might yield more fruitful research findings.

In addition to scientific misunderstanding, contemplatives are subjected to societal misunderstanding and even mistrust. Those who seek a contemplative life must have the strength to go forth alone and accept that conventional society will not appreciate them or their efforts.

Contemplative prayer is work that is both slow and urgent (Peterson, 2003). This slow but urgent work cannot be put off because life in general is deteriorating around us at a rapid pace, and the spiritual life is being compromised, distorted, and degraded even faster. For this reason mystics are needed more than ever before. We must stand fast against the prevailing culture of mindless conformity and light the way toward a better life. For most people, though, slow and urgent are not compatible; they seem like opposites. Contemplative prayer is slow, slow work without shortcuts, and requires endless patience, because impatience prevents contemplation. For too many people, patience is not valued, but speed and multitasking are. Unfortunately, to maintain such constant speed, one must remain on the surface, because depth takes time. The contemplative way of life seems very fragile in this culture of massive technology, arrogant leadership, rampant aggression, and insatiable consumerism, but the work must be done, and urgently.

Chapter Four

Ethics

One of the most valuable contributions a religion makes is its system of morality; it tells its followers how to live their lives. Contemporary Paganism, including Wicca, falls rather short in this regard. In striving to be free of the constraints of conventional religion, any attempt at constructing anything beyond the Wiccan Rede has been rejected as too confining. Here I make an attempt to redress this shortcoming, and in a way that I do not consider too restrictive. We shall examine a new basis for Wiccan morality, and I shall propose a set of values to guide moral reasoning. To begin, we shall consider two contributions from the discipline of psychology that help us understand moral development and behavior.

PSYCHOLOGY OF MORAL BEHAVIOR

Moral Development

Lawrence Kohlberg set forth a structural-developmental theory of moral development that is still consulted today, and is described in varying detail in many texts, so here I shall give a very general overview of his stages. To begin, it is necessary to note that he considered a person's moral development to be dependent on their level of cognitive development.

In early childhood, there is generally little moral thinking done; the child engages in preconventional moral behavior by attempting to avoid punishment while obtaining its own desires as often as possible. The closest to empathy one usually comes at this stage is in the implementation of strict reciprocity. Conventional morality arrives usually around the age of seven or so, when it becomes important for the child to obtain the approval of significant others, and when the child recognizes the importance of law and order. Traditional religion may foster moral development up to the conventional level of moral reasoning, and prevent further development by insisting on upholding its dogma rather than pursuing spiritual enlightenment (Batson, et al, 1993, p. 338). Many people do not develop beyond this level of law and order moral reasoning. Postconventional morality involves recognition of the relative nature of personal values, and the realization of universal ethical principles. Advancement through the stages of this model requires corresponding cognitive advancement in order to be realized. Stages advance by building on the previous stages, which are not lost but incorporated into a larger, more complex understanding that transcends that of the previous stage. Although others have taken exception to this model for varying reasons, it has not been replaced with anything else, and is still a helpful way to understand moral development.

Greater spiritual development can prompt corresponding moral development, due to the expanded vision that emerges, but moral development can progress to higher levels whether the person has a spiritual life or not. We shall see later in this chapter how contemplative practice relates to moral behavior and thought.

Religious Orientation

I include a discussion of religious orientation here because there has been so much work done in this area, with much of it relating to moral behavior. A number of the studies I shall mention require an understanding of religious orientation, so what follows is a brief outline of the theory.

Batson, Schoenrade and Ventis (1993) have posited three ways of being religious, which they refer to as religious orientations: extrinsic, intrinsic, and quest. Put simply, in extrinsic religiousness, the person is involved in religious activities primarily to obtain the personal and social benefits of fitting in to their society. In intrinsic religiousness, the person is involved in religious activities because they believe what their religion teaches and it guides their life. In quest religiousness, the person is searching for God, and asks their own questions while doing so. The quest orientation often does not involve participation in a traditional worship environment, but rather the person follows their own path outside of any recognized religious organization, while those with extrinsic or intrinsic orientations conform to a standard pattern of worship and belief, usually as a member of an organized religion.

It is important to go into a bit more detail regarding the quest orientation, as it has some special and puzzling features that bear on moral functioning. In a study of personality and religious orientation, Francis (2010) found that the quest orientation is not associated with psychoticism, but with introversion and neuroticism, making it quite different from the intrinsic orientation. The extrinsic orientation is associated with neuroticism as well, but finds an association with a traditional church more satisfying, while the quest orientation prefers to contend with spiritual paradox and disquiet on its own terms. Perhaps the most notable feature of the quest orientation is its association with introversion. This was supported by another study (Ross & Francis, 2010) that examined religious orientations in light of Jungian psychological types, and it was found that the quest orientation was strongly related to introverted intuition. It seems the quest orientation is more suited to those individuals with introverted intuition, since they have a preference for discerning meaning in complex situations.

The research, however, is usually beset with various and contradictory findings. Robbins, et al. (2010) found that there is a positive relationship between agreeableness and intrinsic religiosity, but other studies have been unable to find consistent associations between any personality factor and any of the religious orientations (Barrett & Roesch, 2009; Francis, 2010; Francis, Jewell & Robbins, 2010; Francis, Robbins, & Murray, 2010; Ross & Francis, 2010).

These measures of religious orientation are designed to measure different motivations among those who are religious (Francis, 2007). Although the Batson and Ventis theory of religious orientation has perhaps been awarded the most attention in the psychology of religion in recent years, studies do not seem to obtain consistent results, and do not offer a reliable explanation of human religiosity, in spite of the appeal of the theory. Additionally, studies have mainly used college students and church members as subjects, usually taken from Christian schools and churches. Such limited samples present a problem for the application of results, and lead us to question whether the religious orientation measurement scales are meant to measure religiosity itself or merely Christian faith and practice. Francis (2007) states that his improved scale only measures "what it may mean to be religious in a Christian context" (p. 597). In a study (Flere & Lavrič, 2008) of Eastern European Catholics, Muslims, and Orthodox Christians, the scales for intrinsic and extrinsic religiosity simply did not function; there was no measureable difference in results between the two scales in their sample. This does seem to suggest that these constructs only apply to Protestant Christians.

In one study of religious orientation and locus of control (Wong-McDonald & Gorsuch, 2004), the conceptualization of the study variables was skewed toward Christianity, likely resulting in a biased interpretation of findings. The literature is filled with similar findings, so it was some relief to find that one study (Neyrinck, et al., 2010) showed that the three religious orientations do not measure the same thing. According to that study, intrinsic and extrinsic religiosity both seem to measure religious motivation while quest religiosity measures religious cognitive style. This may explain why studies obtain such varied results using these scales. What this study suggests is that the several components of religiosity need to be measured separately to gain a clearer picture of religious functioning.

Ji (2004) gives a wonderful illustration of how we can reconceptualize the structure and measurement of religiosity. Ji shows that when intrinsic religiosity is considered in light of Fowler's (1981) faith development theory, we can see that intrinsic faith can be at either one of the conventional levels, or one of the post-conventional levels, but the intrinsic scale cannot distinguish between the two. This is important because the two developmental levels are different. Conventional faith is exactly that, traditional and conforming, while postconventional faith may appear the same externally, but the believer holds their faith on their own terms and often questions traditional doctrines. Post-conventional faith thinks for itself, while conventional faith follows the teachings of the church without question. Both conventional and postconventional believers can get high scores on the intrinsic religiosity scale, but as each one's faith structure, reasoning, and moral judgment are examined, it becomes clear that their faith is held for very different reasons and in very different ways. Without this distinction, error can be introduced into research findings.

Unfortunately, regarding moral behavior, there is little the research has offered us. Given the discussion above, it is probably not surprising that Hood et al. (2009) assert that there is little association between traditional religiosity and observed ethical behavior. The only positive association they present is that between those with a quest orientation and helping behavior, which they find puzzling since these people do not have traditional religious attitudes. The problem here is that traditional religiosity is strongly associated with conventionality, which, to my mind, prevents people from progressing morally, as those with a quest orientation to religion are better able to do.

Another interesting finding is that as one achieves greater education, moral reasoning becomes less and less affected by one's religious orientation. This may be due to some quality of graduate students that causes them to self-select for graduate school, or it may be due to the experience of graduate education itself. The effect, then, seems to be that the more education one has, the less religiosity informs one's moral decisions (Ji, 2004).

With this contradictory array of empirical results, it is clear that so far the research on religious orientation has not contributed much to our understanding of moral functioning. It is time to have a more complete conception and measurement of religiosity, one that includes development, cognition, motivation, personality, and locus of control, among other areas of functioning. Relying on the religious orientation scale alone is too limiting and misleading.

Contemplation and Moral Behavior

We expect greater spirituality to lead to greater morality; a more intensive prayer life should lead to greater compassion and helping of others. This may not be the case, though, according to one study. Winterowd et al., (2005) produced unexpected findings when they surveyed college students and found that greater levels of anger and its expression were positively associated with greater spirituality, including meditation practice. The researchers believed that this anger may have been an expression of the developmental turmoil college students normally undergo, but it seems to me that the study did not examine all the variables it could have, thereby attaining a fuller picture of what their subjects were experiencing. This study seems to provide either outlying or erroneous data; the results are so different from what is usually found that it is difficult to accept except as the researchers suggest—adolescent developmental turmoil.

Other research has found that spiritual practice in general and meditation in particular fosters prosocial behavior. For one study, Einolf (2013) examined data gathered from 1490 respondents during the 2005 wave of the MacArthur Foundation's Midlife in the United States (MIDUS) study. What this study found is that "… daily spiritual experiences promote helping through the development of extensivity" (Einolf, 2013, p. 83). What this means is that by maintaining a daily spiritual practice, one increases in awareness of the suffering of others and develops a larger sphere of moral concern that can include even the natural and supernatural world. However, because of the self-reported data obtained from telephonic and written questionnaires, social desirability bias likely played some role in the results of this study, so the findings have some limitations.

Nidich et al. (2000), in their excellent discussion of moral development, mention two studies that showed that those who meditate using Transcendental Meditation (TM) exhibited higher levels of moral reasoning than subjects who did not meditate. Additionally, these researchers propose that those who meditate using TM can experience a higher state of consciousness regardless of their current stage of development. Repeated practice of TM can also move a practitioner forward into a more advanced state permanently. The process of TM over time also expands awareness.

The benefits of meditation for prosocial behavior have been extended to children as well. In a social service program for adolescent sex offenders, it was found that yoga training "helped them avoid sexually offending again" (Derezotes, 2000, p. 107). This finding is heartening, but the sample size was very small, and the data were gathered through interviews, so it may be that the children were simply giving the interviewer the response they thought they wanted in the hope of getting through the program more easily or quickly. Nevertheless, a similar result was found with school children of various ages. School meditation was discussed in an article in the *Huffington Post* (Kaleem, 2015), where it was stated that having meditation programs in schools had improved grades and reduced violence.

Perhaps the most solid evidence comes from physiological data. It has been demonstrated that meditation actually changes brain structure (Nidich et al., 2000; Tang, et al., 2010). According to Tang's study, a total of eleven hours' meditation produced changes in subjects' neural pathways associated with the anterior cingulate cortex, an area of the brain associated with self-regulation. The ability to strengthen such pathways through meditation could provide a means for improving self-regulation. This finding suggests that meditation can foster more ethical behavior by improving the connections in the brain that allow a person to behave in a more ethical manner.

Other writings outside the field of psychology are also helpful in understanding the relationship between moral behavior and contemplative life. In a surprising paper, Wright (2006) examined the historical record and found that Japanese Zen masters during the Second World War supported Japan's war effort, making no appeal for peace. The author suggested that this likely came about because Zen enlightenment lacks a moral dimension. If this is so, the Zen practice at that time was merely about achieving detachment, and did not include thoughtful consideration of moral issues or ethical problem solving. What this suggests is that meditation itself may not promote empathy or moral action unless there is a concomitant ethical component to spiritual training.

However, when a moral dimension is included in one's spiritual preparation, quite different results may be obtained. Presenting ideas unlike Wright's above, McRae (2013) offers a Buddhist method of making better moral decisions through the cultivation of equanimity or calm during meditation. This enhanced sense of calm allows one to be free enough to consider moral problems in an impartial and compassionate way, and to adopt a larger sphere of concern. Additionally, one is allowed to accept paradox and exercise greater moral imagination.

This perception has even penetrated into more mundane circles. Writing for the business community in the *Journal of Business Ethics,* La Forge (2000) proposes that meditation supports moral thinking. Although no data were provided, Forbes (2003), in a thoughtful essay, promoted contemplative educational programs to reduce the incidence of standard violent masculinity.

The most satisfying proposal of all, however, comes from Nidich et al. (2000), who point out that unity consciousness achieved through meditation is paralleled by the modern quantum physics view of the universe as an unbroken field of quantum interconnectedness that now replaces the older view of a universe made up of separate and independent parts. I would be glad to see our moral development catch up with our scientific and technological development, because then we could come closer to achieving harmony in the world.

It is my view, based on study and experience, that contemplative practice enlarges our sphere of awareness and ethical concern. Because of this, contemplative practice is salutary not only for individual well-being, but for the improvement of society as well.

PAGAN ETHICS

The application of reason to a belief system prevents those beliefs from contradicting each other. This is one of the values for Wicca of doing theology. Without the foundation of a coherent system of beliefs, there can be no real ethical system. Perhaps it is because of this that Pagans often tolerate a wide array of moral beliefs and practices; they have no firm theological foundation. Pagans are striving to create a new spirituality and way of life, and there is much for them to build upon. Older ethical systems can be incorporated into new Pagan ethics without compromising Pagan spiritual values. Here, I would like to propose an ethical foundation for Wiccans and other Pagans.

Religion has two closely related purposes: to help people achieve union with God, and to teach them how to live meaningfully. In the past, churches focused on teaching people how to live and what to believe by promoting rules and dogma. The churches were too morally undeveloped to allow people to find God on their own, and kept mystics and contemplatives cloistered away from the public eye. Now we need to move ahead. Our technological development has outstripped our moral development, and we are having difficulty coping with our new way of life because of this. Over the last two centuries, we have achieved remarkable technological advances, but we are continuing to live under an archaic moral code and worldview. When we attempt to apply this moral code to contemporary situations, the solutions arrived at do not always succeed. We need to revamp our moral code, and Contemplative Wicca, with its veneration of nature and recognition of the oneness of all things, can help us.

Virtue ethics are the basis of contemporary Pagan ethics (Kraemer, 2012, p. 97). Virtue ethics are based on the classical ethics of Aristotle and other Greek philosophers, or on other ancient teachings such as traditional Germanic virtues. Unfortunately, these ethical systems come from a tribal perspective and are concerned with how males should live a good life, with a great deal of emphasis on individual honor and courage, and no discussion of compassion that I can find. That is because in classical times, compassion was not considered a virtue (Casey, 1990). Today, we are more concerned with empathy and compassion. To me, it seems that we have evolved beyond tribalism and an ethic of virtues, and that trying to revive classical virtues as a basis for moral thought is not only regressive but also irrelevant. Humanity has experienced the teachings of great spiritual masters, such as the Buddha and the Christ, which offer a universalizing worldview, and these teachings should not be abandoned without careful examination.

More advanced notions of how to treat each other should be retained and incorporated regardless of source, rather than, merely for the sake of religious consistency, reviving a system that has no relevance for modern life and does not foster further progress. Compassion for all life requires a much larger worldview than that offered by a tribal system of ethics. We need a larger worldview than that provided by the current established religions as well, so we must move forward, taking what is worthwhile and leaving the irrelevant behind.

Using the term "virtues" is also misleading, and I prefer to think of "values" instead. "Virtues" seems to imply a personal accomplishment, while "values" implies a guide for living. I believe the focus of striving to live according to values is better than the focus of living a virtuous life because the traditional virtuous life seems too concerned with achieving personal honor, while living according to values seems more concerned with achieving personal and social harmony and justice. After all, the purpose of ethics and morality today is to discover how to live well together, not how to live well as an individual.

Harrow (in Lewis, 1996, pp. 20-21) says that the most important idea Pagans can offer society is the knowledge that we can cause suffering when we want more than our share of the Earth's resources, and when others and the Earth suffer, we suffer as well, because we are all one. Paganism celebrates variety, which also fosters the conviction that we are all one (York, 2003, p. 158). Contemplative prayer allows us to see that the variety found in nature and in human society is just different manifestations of the essential unity that binds us all. When we fully realize that we are all one, we can begin to live in balance.

Following rules woodenly is not a firm foundation for moral behavior, but living according to values is, because it requires an understanding of the purpose of the rules and of the goals humans are trying to accomplish as a society. Once a person can see God in the universe, and treat all things as holy, then an external moral imperative is no longer needed (Maxwell, 2003, p. 273). This is the goal we must move toward, to have our values internalized, and therefore more firmly lived. There is still a need for rules for most people, however, because until morality is internalized as deeply held values, external rules are required to guide behavior.

The Wiccan Rede

Wicca, lacking a doctrine of sin, does not offer commandments, outside of the traditional admonition, "harm none, and do what you will." It is the very simplicity of this rule that precludes any misunderstanding or prevarication. It is absolutely clear—do no harm. This is refreshing and a great improvement over having a multitude of complex laws that allow for as many interpretations and obfuscations as there are readers of the law. As legal interpretations accumulate, how can they all be remembered or applied with precision in changing circumstances? New laws and new interpretations must be formulated to handle new situations, and the problem only increases. When judges try to decide how to treat a case brought before them, the best thing to do is to simply consider how to do no harm and benefit both parties, rather than decide where the guilt lies and who should be punished.

Nevertheless, while "do no harm" may provide a good foundation for our morality, the guidance it provides is limited. The Rede only shows enlightened hedonism, not advanced moral development, and rather than simply avoiding the doing of harm,

72

attempting to actively engage in right living is better. A more positive notion of diligently promoting the common good is more proactive, leading us to work to make changes for the better. Merely following the traditional rule would not bring forward much change, and would allow people to refrain from intervening in helpful ways. One's relationship with the material world is sacred; therefore, to respect the divinity in the world and others, one must live rightly in the world and with each other (York, 2003, p. 157). This principle should lead us to promote good actively, rather than remaining satisfied with merely refraining from evil.

Contemplative spirituality can be used by some as an escape from the world, an excuse to accept God's will and retreat into solitude, offering little or no assistance to others. One can also use one's spiritual accomplishments to aggrandize oneself and have power over others (O'Connor, 2002, p.143). Instead, contemplative life and prayer should show us how to live rightly. It is not always clear how to act, and we require moral imagination to see what is at stake in a given situation and how best to resolve it. Wooden application of rules does not always work, and it is not always clear which principles or "rules" to apply. It is often necessary to think outside the usual categories to solve a problem, and to do this we need to understand the goals of the rules, not just the rules themselves. The greater our spiritual understanding, and the greater knowledge and insight we have, the greater the likelihood that we can make better moral decisions. This level of wisdom is achieved over many years of experience and effort in contemplative prayer as well as in daily living.

Perceiving all creation as One with God can foster a sense of compassion for all and desire to help others, including the environment (Carpenter, 2014, p. 8). In a recent study (Garfield, 2014), spiritual Oneness, based on contemplative spirituality, was found to be a better predictor of pro-environmental attitudes and behavior than traditional religiousness. What we can conclude from this is that contemplative prayer, beliefs, and values can lead to more genuine good than churchgoing alone. Since Oneness belief is the core of a monotheistic or a panentheistic spirituality, its measurement is extremely important for the future study of religion as it likely can show the salutary aspects of religiosity better than all the other measures used heretofore.

Free Will

In Western society, it is believed that an adult person is responsible for their behavior, and this belief informs our ethical and justice systems. It is sadly a fallacy, as people have much less free will than they are given credit for. The range of situations that present themselves to a person and the range of choices they can make are limited by their personal and environmental circumstances, such as level of education and degree of insight. We can be responsible to the greatest extent for carefully considered decisions we have taken time to make. Decisions thrust upon us by circumstances that are out of our control are much harder to manage, and therefore to have responsibility for. Nevertheless, people have always judged the right and wrong of people's behavior in light of their belief in free will.

Our notions of free will may arise from some variant of the fundamental attribution error. The fundamental attribution error is the bias we in the West have to believe others' behavior is caused by their personality rather than by the pressure of the situation they are in. This is because during our development as a society we found it more important to classify persons than situations, so our process of attribution tends to give more weight to personal causes of behavior and less to situational causes. This is a robust finding in many studies. Because individual behavior is far more salient to Western people than circumstances, we have come to believe that individuals are responsible for their actions; that they choose to do what they do. This is so even though we know our own behavior is often constrained by events. This belief in human free will has informed all of our social interactions, especially our judicial and penal systems, leading to much unfair treatment of each other, and blighting society with unnecessary suffering. Science helps us see how our behavior is really caused, and can help show us the way to improve our treatment of each other.

People become who they are and behave the way they do based on their genetic inheritance and their environment. Within these parameters, there is a great amount of flexibility and conscious choice in behavior and personality, but there are limits. A person with genes for being short will never be tall, even in an optimal environment of good health, exercise, and diet. A person with genes for being tall may be tall if provided with an adequate environment while growing, but would be taller still if raised in an optimal environment, with the best diet, exercise, and health care. Certain environments allow certain genes to be expressed fully, while other environments prevent their expression or subdue it. Individuals have no control over either who their parents are or the environment they are raised in. By the time they are self-aware enough to take some charge of their lives, their early childhood is over and much of their life and personality is set. As Michaelson (2009, p. 209-213) points out, free will is just an illusion.

How can a poor person possibly behave in the same way as an affluent person? Their education and standard of living are much less than that of the wealthy person, and their range of choices is severely limited. They live their lives at a subsistence level. Growing up with no heat, irregular food, little or no supervision, and the tumult of criminal or drug-dependent caregivers often leads to a traumatized personality and criminal behavior. Those with this kind of background likely will grow up with a certain repertoire of behaviors, and will live in a circle of people that will preclude them from ever having financial or social success. To hold them responsible for their behavior seems exceedingly unfair and shortsighted. Where was their modeling? What opportunities did they have to do otherwise than they did?

A recent study (Noble, 2015) discovered that there is a strong association between poverty and brain size in children: the poorer the family, the smaller the brain size and the lower the level of cognitive function of the child. Since poverty is the result of social injustice, whose fault is it that so many poor are so disadvantaged that they turn to crime? It is very easy to lay moral and legal blame on another, but some are simply squeezed out of the benefits others take for granted, and cannot be held to the same standards as others who have led a different life with greater privileges. Mercy can be practiced more easily if we understand that there is no free will, only genetics and environment that shape us, leaving less to individual choice than we think.

It is important to consider this in legal situations. When a person is brought to trial, they may be judged guilty of the crime they are accused of, but are they really responsible for their actions? Americans like to think that people have access to a full range of education and resources, supported by public taxes. This is not the case, as we all know. There are areas of the country where the economy is simply less robust, there are fewer amenities, the school districts are poorly supplied, and the people earn a lower wage than in more affluent areas. This is clearly illustrated by a report released by the National Association of Counties (Istrate & Knudsen, 2016) on county economies in 2015, which stated that only 7 percent of county economies had completely recovered from the recession of 2008, while 16 percent had not recovered at all, leaving most counties only partially recovered. They also reported that 28 percent of county economies experienced declining wages even though productivity increased, illustrating that employers are managing to get their pound (or more) of flesh with only the threat of joblessness to motivate workers. And, according to the Public Religion Research Institute (Jones et al., 2015), 72 percent of Americans consider the US still to be in recession, indicating that many people have been living directly with these numbers, and drawing their own conclusions. These data clearly show the deep economic disparity present in the United States.

When a person is struggling to survive, the stress level is nearly unbearable, and it is difficult to behave with courtesy and to exert the self-control of a person whose basic needs are met. When such a person is faced with someone they perceive to be affluent, and they are very conscious of the injustice against them, how could they feel it wrong to take from the one who is so well off they could not feel the loss very keenly? Among the poor, the constant reinforcement of their worthlessness simply supports their predation of others. Life is desperate, and one must survive. They fight and rob because they do not have any other behavior available to them to express their feelings or take action against their troubles. Prosecuting and punishing such people is very similar to placing the poor is debtors' prison until their debts are paid.

Instead of a war on crime, there should be a war on ignorance. More schools should be built instead of prisons, and more care should be taken to fit people for a productive life. There are very few truly bad people, but there are many who are not living in their proper place in life, and cannot be expected to contribute to their full potential. Often they detract from the harmony of society by engaging in criminal or other dysfunctional behavior, and the only lasting way to combat this is to realize that everyone can contribute something to society, and to expend every effort to help people live up to their potential. Punishing people for not doing well in a hopeless situation is nothing but unjust.

What this means spiritually is that there is no room for a doctrine of sin. Since we have so little control in life, how can we be held culpable? How can God consider us responsible for behavior that is conditioned in us? None of us can act selflessly or beneficially all the time, and even the mildest person will fight when pressed hard enough. As long as people attempt to live harmoniously with others and to do no harm, it is sufficient. It seems far too petty for God to maintain a ledger of offences on each person and exact eternal punishment for infractions against some impossible standard. We are none of us here by choice, and as long as we do the best we can with what we have, it is reasonable to assume that we are in God's grace.

To conclude this section, it is necessary to mention forgiveness. Michaelson (2009, p. 187) points out that if God is everywhere, then whom are we to forgive? What is there to forgive? If we are all part of God, then it's God who has wronged you, God who has been wronged, God who is wronging Itself. It seems that forgiveness is irrelevant, since we are all One.

VALUES

Just as we are unable to think and feel without our bodies, we are unable to find meaning without our spiritual lives. Our society with its Protestant work ethic and capitalist material values denies this and expects us to forego our total selves for a partial one. As we see every day, though, this no longer works and we need to adopt new values in order to survive. We need a moral revolution, and the new values necessary to lead it. Success needs to be redefined as the promotion of the common good, as self-sacrifice, as sharing and collaboration rather than as a few heroic winners getting more than the losers who make up the majority. In a new, just, and sustainable society, there would be no winners or losers. Everyone would make their contribution and participate in the general well-being and plenty. The goal of life should not be economic success but happiness, beauty, peace, and well-being. Our task as a civilization is to help everyone fit in, and assure well-being for all by providing basic necessities. Here, I provide a discussion of Pagan values that would help to accomplish this.

Oneness

This is the primary value, guiding all the others. When we can see that we are all One, and God is everywhere, then how can we intentionally cause harm? The conviction that we are all one allows us to see that we can indeed do no other than live in harmony with each other and the rest of creation. We are part of nature and all life has value because God is everywhere and in all things. If we reverence everyone and everything, how can we countenance any harm to others, even nonsentient others?

We also are called to union with God, which is achieved through prayer and right living. Our prayer should continue throughout the day, not just at set prayer times or festivals, so that our whole day is lived as a prayer. A prayerful awareness of the Divine makes each day into a prayer, even when we are engaged in mundane tasks. This awareness supports us as we strive to live rightly.

Cooperation and peace

The time for aggression is over. There is no place left to conquer, except space, which may be beyond our conquering. Life has become far more predictable and less dangerous than it was for our ancestors, and aggression is now a liability. Behaviors that once were lauded in a warrior now get a person arrested. Steven Hawking pointed this out in an article in the *Independent*.

> "The human failing I would most like to correct is aggression," the astrophysicist said. "It may have had survival advantage in caveman days, to get more food, territory or a partner with whom to reproduce, but now it threatens to destroy us all." The human quality the scientist would most like to magnify was empathy. "It brings us together in a peaceful loving state." (Clark, 2015)

Aggression should be channeled into harmless pursuits like sports, and aggressive people should not run things unchecked. Cooperation, rather than competition, should be fostered early in life. The great challenge of our lives should be to discern how to achieve peace: not just the absence of war, but true cooperation between people and between people and the environment so that all benefit. This will allow us to live in greater harmony with all who share the planet with us, and will enable us to enjoy greater quality of life.

Unity and cooperation allow us to accomplish things we could never accomplish alone, and give us a cohesiveness that prevents conflict. Equitable sharing of resources and fair treatment of each other ensure everyone's well-being and prevent aggression.

Sharing and universal welfare

Society needs a system of regulation or checks and balances to offer equity to all and assure productivity and safety. There should be no political parties or nationalist ideology, just an impartial government that provides regulation and oversight, and assures equity, safety, and the smooth running of society. Society should provide education, healthcare, shelter, utilities (sanitation, water, and energy), communication, transportation, food, clothing (basic clothing available to all), safety, and research; to name the most basic services. There would be no need for insurance, politicians, or lawyers, and courts would be supplanted by mediators or regulators. This would work if we could replace competition with cooperation. Our current society values only competition; those who succeed are extolled and those who cannot compete are left behind. It is telling that bees, one of the most cooperative species and upon whose labor we depend so utterly, are dying out due to the effects of our competitive society, as we seek ever-larger crop yields.

Understanding and tolerance

Cooperation and sharing can be fostered best by promoting the understanding of others and the world around us. Travel should become easier so people can come to know one another and experience varying environments. We have access to information of great variety and scope; we can communicate with others almost anywhere, and we can have this communication instantly. This brings us very close to others even when physically distant, and engenders a greater sense of fellowship than happens when people are considered to be strangers. We can use this ability to achieve greater tolerance of differences and make our world more like a community than a far-flung assemblage of separate states populated by distant strangers. We can live harmoniously when we not only tolerate but understand and make use of our diversity.

In addition to travel and communication, education is another, and perhaps the best, weapon against intolerance and conflict.

Education

Education can promote tolerance and help us to live in greater happiness and productivity, allowing all to be constructively employed to the best of their ability, and moving our civilization ahead. Freedom to pursue our own individuality is necessary if we are to make the maximum contribution to society and find real satisfaction in life. Education needs to focus on developing the unique strengths of individuals so they can do the work they are meant to do rather than forcing them into a stifling conformity that ultimately causes more harm than good. Crowding young children into schools where the students vastly outnumber the teachers is not conducive to learning or prosocial development. Students need more individual attention and assistance than is provided in traditional classrooms, and the efficiency of the school system provides only the short-term benefits of crowd management. In the long term, it would be far more beneficial to have children attended to individually by adults than to leave them to each other's influence so much of the time. Children need the guidance of adults, and are unable to learn much of value from each other. If a child is guided by a sympathetic and capable adult, their learning and development can progress faster than if they are forced to wait for the rest of the group, or if they are constantly struggling to keep up. Instruction tailored to the personality and abilities of the child would be more effective and ultimately would help provide the child with a more satisfying and productive life doing work that they can do well and enjoy.

Beauty

Many people find it easy to perceive the Divine through a beautiful sunset or the song of a bird. Beauty is positive and uplifting and can give us a sense of the transcendent.

Beauty also promotes happiness and helps us feel better about ourselves and our surroundings. If we live in a well-kept and attractive place, we have a more positive outlook than if we live in a place that is shabby, unsafe, or uncomfortable. Most people know that they feel better about themselves if they make themselves attractive. Beauty seems to indicate to us that the beautiful thing is worthwhile and valued. Beauty should be sought because it has so many benefits, and its appreciation should be fostered through education.

Pagans generally consider pleasure to be a human birthright (Kraemer, 2012, p. 83), and certainly there are types of pleasure that can foster a religious or numinous experience. In the Middle Ages, going to church afforded a downtrodden populace one of the very few experiences of beauty they had. The glorious music, fragrant incense, and magnificent churches took these people up out of their grim daily existence to a special experience of beauty that helped to bring them closer to God. This type of aesthetic pleasure can be found whenever we encounter overwhelming beauty, and that beauty can provide a significant spiritual experience. Beauty is an important part of spiritual practice because of the power it has to show us God, in addition to providing pleasure. Pleasure can result from beauty as well as other causes, but can frequently be meaningless unless it has a more significant foundation. It is for this reason I suggest that beauty, because it is such an important, meaningful, and powerful foundation, should be included in our spiritual practice, as well as in the rest of our lives and in our environments.

Progress

Society must move forward. We cannot cling to useless or harmful traditions and technologies. Humans need a challenge, and discovery and innovation are compelling challenges that can provide great benefits to all. Improvements in science and other fields enable us to live more effectively in the world, and increase our happiness. If progress and change are not embraced, then society stagnates.

Spirituality must progress too. Prophets and mystics can see that a new world is possible if people put spiritual values first, but the wealthy refuse to pay the price and the poor are too overwhelmed to envision it. Contemplatives move human spirituality ahead. By continuing to call out to others and lead the way into the future, contemplatives can eventually elevate human consciousness to the point that people will no longer need to wage war and engage in mutual exploitation. Perhaps this, along with recent technological and social changes, will help humanity to make the necessary major leap forward.

Rights and Responsibilities

My promotion of social justice notwithstanding, it therefore truly seems to me that we have no real rights at all, only privileges and responsibilities. The ideas I have recently explored have already clarified that life itself is a privilege; many do not enjoy a full life but die of natural causes while still young, so how can it be a universal right? As I stated to some extent when discussing free will, many of the things we consider rights simply cannot be provided when society or the environment collapses. There are many who are deprived of basic necessities because they live in an area devastated by environmental or other calamity and their "rights" cannot be upheld. This happens so frequently that basic things like clean water really are a privilege. We should provide people with physical and social benefits such as health care and education not because it is their right, but because it is the right thing to do.

The overwhelming conclusion, therefore, is that those who do have more privileges also have more responsibilities. We all have the responsibility to live rightly, as best we can in our circumstances, but those who have more have the responsibility to help those less fortunate. Fulfilling our responsibilities to each other and the environment is also a privilege because it is a part of life that we should be glad to see through because we are all One. When we can embrace each other and the world because we are all One, then the enforcement of legislated rights eventually will not be necessary.

Gratitude

Gratitude is closely related to this. Gratitude gives us a better perspective on life and prevents us from becoming too arrogant. When we understand that we are all One, we understand that our privileges are not special, and that we may suffer just like anyone else. Nothing in life is guaranteed, and it is important to realize that whatever good we have is a blessing, and to be grateful. When we see that life is a privilege, we can find joy where we would not otherwise.

CONCLUSION

Except for developmental theories, which show how we grow both spiritually and morally, most psychological research has provided us with little assistance in understanding how people are religious, or how religiosity relates to moral behavior. Some research, however, supports meditation as a salutary activity, promoting spiritual and physical well-being. Meditation also is considered to enlarge the practitioner's awareness and sphere of moral concern.

Pagan ethics are rather haphazard, and would benefit from firm theological support. Pagans must also beware of regressive tendencies to reclaim too much of the ancient past as the ethical guidance it can provide often is irrelevant or even detrimental. We must look forward; keep what is worth keeping from the past, and devise new ways to live in a new world, based on our belief in Oneness.

One of the things not worth keeping is the belief in free will. Our justice systems and personal interactions need to be revised with the understanding that personal responsibility is far less than has been heretofore supposed, and should be based on helping people to make a contribution to society rather than establishing guilt and punishment.

I have put forth Oneness, cooperation, peace, sharing and universal welfare, understanding and tolerance, education, beauty, progress, responsibility and gratitude as values to guide our behavior and thinking, and to remake the world. These values have arisen through theological reflection on contemplative experience, and are not new or unique to Contemplative Wicca. They nonetheless need to be articulated as we must move forward into a more complete and coherent Pagan theology that will guide our lives and reshape society for a new world. I offer these ideas in the hope that this new world will be happier, and blessed with more grace than we have enjoyed of late.

Prayer

Prayer is active communion with God. It can take any number of forms, as each person relates to God in their own way, and can be done while engaged in other activities. Prayer can be formal, as in group rituals, or informal, as when one has a spontaneous, private conversation with God. As embodied persons, we tend to follow the traditions we are familiar with, because they have acquired meaning for us through repeated use (Michaelson, 2009, p. 4), and they are necessary to conduct community prayer and ritual. Mystics are no different, and usually adopt the theology of their professed religion, but see in it a depth and richness ordinary people don't (Underhill, 1974, p. 125). "…mysticism blurs the boundaries which religion seeks to enforce" (Michaelson, 2009, p. 2), thus rendering the dogmas and rules of particular religions irrelevant to contemplatives. God is inferred from the experience of mystical prayer, and it may be that mystical experience began the social phenomenon of religion in ancient times. Mysticism has a universal core that transcends cultures and individuals, and provides the same basic experience worldwide for all mystics. Because contemplatives live at the center where the universal truths are without the encumbrance of specific cultural and doctrinal restrictions, they can unite the world. An integrated spirituality would build on this universal core, while accepting the various cultural expressions of mysticism (Maxwell, 2003, p. 266). Contemplative Wicca particularly is suited to this task.

What distinguishes humans from other creatures is the condition of being both finite and infinite, of having awareness of transcendence even while being physical. Because of this duality in humans, people find their deepest needs unmet in the physical world. Without a relationship with God, human wholeness or integration is impossible (Harrison, 1999, p. 431). In the view of Hans Urs von Balthasar, a person becomes whole or holy by engaging in contemplative prayer, where one receives one's identity, and mission or task from God, and by living up to this task (Harrison, 1999). This is the great power of contemplative prayer, but taking the path of contemplation to the Divine is a lengthy process, and not always satisfying. Here we shall look at various types of prayer and even examine magic.

TYPES OF PRAYER

Prayer can be formal or informal, intercessory or devotional, prayed in a group or alone. Although the boundaries between each type of prayer are very permeable, it is helpful to understand their differences in order to grasp the significance of contemplative practice. Let us examine each type.

Formal prayer or ritual is most often done in groups, but ritual can also be practiced when alone. It generally involves the performance of a series of set actions and a series of set prayers, and can be used in a variety of ways. Formal, group prayer, such as church or temple worship services, can be bland and easily ignored, or prayed with intercessory or devotional fervor. Large group rituals can also be used as opportunities for contemplative attention to the words used or the music heard, and can help in achieving contact with the sacred. In Wiccan contemplative practice, ritual is still used, but the ritual is quiet, with more time spent in meditation and less time in ritual acts. Wiccan contemplative ritual could include circle casting, a devotional reading, meditation, and opening the circle, for example. Ritual is important because it makes sacred space more tangible. It is important to note that while ritual is often shared with others, meditation, even when done in a group, is essentially solitary.

Informal prayer lacks a set format of actions or prayers, and can be practiced in groups or alone. Informal prayer involves the person or group praying naturally, in their own words, or even performing a spontaneous ritual. Such prayer can be devotional or intercessory.

Intercessory prayer involves the devotee simply asking, or in some cases, begging, for what is wanted or needed, for example, "Please get me this new job" or "Please make my child well." People will sometimes even bargain with God to entice It to give them what they want ("I'll go to church every Sunday if You let me close this important business deal"). This type of prayer involves little listening and a great deal of monologing, while contemplative prayer involves a quiet listening for any message God may send. Intercessory prayer can be formal or informal in structure.

Devotional prayer is turning one's attention to the Deity with adoration. Intercession is not included; rather, devotional prayer can involve the reading of scriptures or other devotional materials, as well as ritual. Devotional prayer can also be spontaneous and informal, even wordless. An example of this is when we pause on a walk to gaze at a snow-capped peak, or watch a herd of deer run across a meadow, and experience awe, joy, and gratitude. Mystical prayer is generally devotional in intent.

Mystical prayer is intended to bring the practitioner to a numinous, unitive meeting with God. Mystical prayer uses either contemplative or ecstatic methods, and can result in either an immanent, personal experience of God, or a transcendent experience with a more impersonal Oneness (Holm, 1982). An immanent experience can be an intimate encounter with God as lover, friend, brother, or some other direct, deeply personal experience of God, while devotees often describe a transcendent experience as an experience of the Void, or of God as Other, the Absolute, or Ultimate Reality. Such encounters with the Holy are ineffable, and the words chosen to describe them are necessarily inadequate, but they at least partially convey the awesome nature of mystical experience. Divine union is the ultimate goal of prayer and indeed, both contemplative and ecstatic methods, as well as immanent and transcendent experiences, are equally valid. Union with God, although difficult to describe, always is seen as positive and life-enhancing, and has been sought by devotees of all faiths for millennia. Many do not achieve divine union, but prayer enhances the openness and ability of the person to accept such an experience when it is given.

Ecstatic prayer is the type of prayer usually favored by Pagans, involving music, dancing, and ritual. In this type of prayer, the devotee can be transported to awareness of the Divine through physical exertion and excessive sensory input. Some shamanic techniques fall into this category. Contemplative prayer, or meditation, is often done in silence, or at least quietly, and often alone. Ecstatic and contemplative prayers are mutually exclusive. Although contemplation can be accomplished using a sacred image to focus on, or quiet music or chanting, the level of activity during ecstatic prayer is greater and leads the devotee to God through a very different path than contemplation, which requires quiet and stillness. Zen walking meditation or yoga are examples of the few active contemplative techniques that are commonly used, and adept practitioners can continue their contemplation even during their everyday activities.

The mystical state can be described using William James' (1958, p. 292) four criteria: ineffability, noetic quality, transience, and passivity. Such experiences of Oneness are usually difficult to explain to the uninitiated, and mystics' descriptions of their experiences seem more akin to feeling states. Nevertheless, the experience has a noetic quality, providing the practitioner with illumination and new understanding, and knowledge that is authoritative and transformative. Both ineffability and noesis are James' main requirements for an experience to be considered mystical. He also points out that mystical states cannot be maintained for very great lengths of time, and that the experience itself involves being taken up by a greater power. The first is not true for all, as some accomplished contemplatives are able to keep a mystical awareness at all times, and the second occurs only in trance states, or experiences of deep contemplation. James (1958, p. 321) considers the attainment of Oneness to be the great mystical achievement, which is the same regardless of time or place or creed. Most mystics have provided startlingly similar reports of unity with the Absolute, and this similarity should indicate to us that they have found Ultimate Truth through mystical prayer.

The unique and valid aspect of mysticism is the individual's direct experience of God (Underhill, 1974, p. 102), which also provides the most compelling evidence for the existence of God. According to Michaelson (2009, p. 168, 221), contemplative prayer and meditation is the way to experience the infinite expanse of Being and space/time, and to see oneself as an inseparable part of It. It is this experience of contemplative prayer and meditation that engenders a harmony between the mystic and the rest of creation (Underhill, 1974, p. 258) and prevents the hierarchical thinking that leads to aggression and oppression (Christ, 1997, p. 100).

MEDITATION METHOD: SIMPLE PRAYER

I advocate simple prayer. Although the meditation method I encourage is somewhat similar to the empty mind of Zen, lengthy training is not necessary in order to pray successfully. Instead of anything too severe or complex, I suggest a simple quiet sitting, a careful listening for the voice of God. This is simple indeed, but very difficult to do. It requires stilling the thoughts and body, and focusing on the quiet. Attending to the quiet allows us to hear, which is one of the most important aspects of prayer. The voice of God can be small and difficult to discern; it requires our undivided attention. God speaks to us seldom, but it behooves us to be listening when It does.

The best way to do this is to have a special place to sit that is quiet and allows you to clear your mind. Distractions must be eliminated and a clear period of time alone must be set aside for this activity. Some time should be spent every day in meditation, shorter ten to fifteen minute periods at first, then longer times, up to half an hour, can be spent. This is usually sufficient, especially for beginners, but as one becomes more adept, one can spend even longer times meditating.

Beginners should start their practice with a meditation teacher, or by attending a class or a Zendo, for example. Group meditation can be very powerful and provide guidance for those starting out. Care must be taken when beginning meditation, as it can become easy to lose oneself without proper training and focus. As one's skill increases, it becomes easier to meditate in a variety of environments, even busy airports.

Under no circumstances do I recommend the use of drugs. Although this is popular among some Pagans, particularly among those following certain indigenous traditions, it is altogether unnecessary. God is there regardless, and we can hear It if we simply listen. Similarly, I do not recommend the use of physical privation or other extreme ascetic methods to alter consciousness. Unsought extreme experiences, however, can occasionally offer us an opportunity to see or hear God in a powerful way because our senses and awareness have been shifted away from their usual path, by, for example, illness, injury, or loss. A sufficient number of such experiences come to us without any seeking on our part. It is up to us to use them for listening and learning to the best of our ability.

MAKING SACRED SPACE AND RITUAL

To perceive the Absolute, one must alter consciousness slightly (Underhill, 1974, p. 30). Sacred space can be made anywhere, with or without the use of ritual implements, and putting oneself in sacred space helps to alter consciousness sufficiently to make it easier to perceive the Divine. The use of ritual and the making of sacred space help us to focus our prayer, and can provide a platform for group celebrations. The use of a simple ritual such as lighting candles and calling the directions can put your mind in a more receptive state for listening to God by making tangibly sacred the time and place where you are.

Of course, one does not "make" sacred space, as it is there

regardless of what we do. When we call the directions or perform any other similar ritual, we are merely allowing ourselves to recognize the sacredness of all space, and especially the sacredness of the place and time we are to spend in prayer. Oneness shows us that the Earth is sacred, and we are sacred, so all we need to do is make ourselves aware of this.

For Sabbats and Moons, it is appropriate and enjoyable to set up the altar, cast a circle, and perform some simple ritual that helps you to enter sacred space and enables you to listen better. Such circles can be celebrated alone on holydays, and solitaries have a tradition of such ritual circles. Any simple ritual to set up the sacred space can be sufficient to prepare you for your meditation and allow you to listen to God. It must be noted, though, that casting a ritual circle is not necessary to meditate. Meditation can be done any time without any ritual at all; all that is required is to attend to God.

MAGIC

The use of magic is considered by most to be an integral part of witchcraft, therefore a clear definition of and parameters for magic are in order. For Contemplative Wicca, magic is not necessary, and not advised. The use of magic proposed below is perhaps insufficient for many people, but the purpose of Contemplative Wicca is spiritual growth rather than power.

Bonewits (1989, p. 24) says that there is no clear division between mysticism and magic; but points out that magic is directed outward toward practical ends while mysticism is directed inward toward spiritual attainment. Ritual is used in both endeavors, and can give them a similar appearance (Bonewits, 1989, p.220). He states that magic is the use of paranormal powers for concrete ends; more specifically, the conscious direction of personal energy toward other energy patterns, either animate or inanimate, with the intention of altering them toward one's own goals (Bonewits, 1989, p. 258), while mysticism is the use of personal energy for spiritual purposes (Bonewits, 1989, p. 260).

Although Bonewits' definition is basically correct, Underhill clarifies the distinction between magic and mysticism more accurately. Real magic is the superficial manifestation of supernatural power attained through harmony with the Divine or Absolute. It is attained in the last stages of mystical development, by very few, or by those especially gifted with paranormal or supernatural abilities. Magic and mysticism are on the same continuum, or at least are related, and they veil the same ineffable truths, although their practitioners do not share the same conscious goals (Underhill, 1974, p. 163). Ordinarily, magic is sought rather than successfully practiced, and occultists' and magicians' main goal is personal power rather than being, or union with the Divine (Underhill, 1974, p. 162). Underhill states that in order to avoid profane magic and attain true mystical union with God, the desire to be should precede the desire for knowledge or power (Underhill, 1974, p.151). The problem with nonreligious magic is that doing or willing comes first, and there may be no system of morality guiding it. To magically will may be well if it is guided by a moral system and has a spiritual foundation, but there is a danger of upsetting the natural balance in trying to use magic for personal ends. Individuals do not have the breadth and depth of awareness and understanding that would enable them to exert magical power over others safely; when one has power, it is too easy to consider only selfish ends and ignore the far-reaching consequences. What people usually see of magic are just the superficial effects, and the power is what they are attracted to. They do not understand or accept that such power requires real work over an extended period of time in order to develop the necessary spiritual and moral base, as well as emotional and intellectual strength and experience. As stated above, this is attained by very few, and most magical practitioners are motivated by the desire for power.

Underhill's three axioms of magic delineate the similarities and the differences between magic and mysticism with helpful detail.

1 – Astral Light: This is the principle that there is a supernatural plane, and a higher level of consciousness; and that this higher plane is the force connecting everything; the source of life. This higher plane is real, and can be reached directly from our own mundane level of existence. This is common and essential to both magic and mysticism, as in mystical or contemplative prayer one attempts to directly connect with God. It is the source of the magician's power, as well as the power of the mystic (Underhill, 1974, p. 154+). It may provide the supernatural or psychic powers for those few blessed with them. Contemplatives may consider this to be God.

2 – Development of the Will: This principle postulates "the limitless power of the disciplined human will." Both magic and mysticism promote discipline. Magicians advocate mental practice and the use of ritual, rigorously applied to develop the powers of apprehension and supernatural abilities and skills for the practice of magic. This is as in mysticism, where one meditates, and follows religious rituals and practices in order to develop an apprehension of the Divine. These practices help attain the ecstatic or contemplative state, and enable one's connection with the Divine. Mystics and magicians use words and objects (gazing crystals, statues, etc.) to help focus the energy and the mind and achieve the desired altered state, but the adept can eventually dispense with such outward assistance (Underhill, 1974, p. 156-159). The purpose of this discipline is to hone the latent natural powers of the practitioner, making them supernatural, thus enabling them to see the Divine or connect to the Astral Light. Such discipline and training enabled magicians to effectively wield their powers of suggestion and hypnotism to change the perceptions of their students and their audience. Ancient occultists had power and an evil reputation because they used psychology before its time (Underhill, 1974, p.161) in order to take advantage of the credulous. The key difference between the magus and the mystic is in the purpose of the discipline. The magus desires to know and do, while the mystic merely desires to be; the magus seeks power over others while the mystic seeks union with God.

3 – Analogy: The principle of analogy states that as it is above, so it is below; the supernatural is mirrored in the mundane. According to Underhill, this is where magic fails and diverges from mysticism (Underhill, 1974, p. 159+). This assumption presumes a rather Christian worldview, with heaven and earth and a transcendent God. Since there is no heaven as such, there is no "above" for "below" to follow. Although this was a popular belief in ancient times, it is not seriously considered today. It is in this area that science has supplanted both magic and religion, and people now turn to science for reliable information about the world. Additionally, and most importantly, occultists' and magicians' main goal is attaining power and control rather than being, or connecting with the Divine (Underhill, 1974, p. 162). Although there are those who have attained some magical skill, when the practitioner is lacking the essential spiritual core, despite all her apparent power, she has not achieved connection with the Divine. "...the mere transcending of phenomena does not entail the attainment of the Absolute" (Underhill, 1974, p. 151).

Although *Mysticism* is perhaps the standard text on the subject, it is not truly comprehensive. Underhill discussed mysticism and magic with a decidedly Western viewpoint; she refers only to the three major Western religions, primarily Christianity, depriving her readers of the benefit derived from the great wealth of Eastern knowledge and practice.

The most common and benign type of magic, the magic we have all witnessed and participated in, is ritual magic. This is usually performed by the celebrant at a house of worship, and aids in the creation of sacred space. Such ritual acts are magic for the purposes of altering consciousness, and to create sacred space in order to allow one to apprehend the Divine (Underhill, 1974, p. 161). Although the use of ritual is primitive, it persists to this day because it does work, not to control the gods, but to alter our awareness. This is the best use of magic, as it does not involve the attempt to control others, only oneself.

The only other type of magic I advocate is visualization, which is discussed below. When practicing any type of magic, even the most benign, one must remember the principle that whatever energy one sends out, it will return to the sender threefold. This is a sobering truth that must guide all practice of magic, and indeed, all of our actions. It must also be remembered that circumventing nature is not advised, as the consequences are too far-reaching to be fully considered and controlled.

VISUALIZATION

Visualization is a powerful technique that can be considered both a type of prayer and a way of practicing magic. As a type of prayer, it would more truly be considered a sort of intercessory prayer, as it involves the visualization of what the practitioner desires to accomplish. Rather than a blatant asking of God for what they wish to obtain, it involves instead a focusing of the mind and the attention, allowing the practitioner to see opportunities to accomplish this thing, which were not previously apparent. Visualization can also aid in contemplative prayer by allowing the practitioner to focus on a religious image. The focus that this accomplishes can be helpful in achieving a deeper meditative state.

As magic, Visualization can be used to great effect in the same way as described above for intercessory prayer. One simply holds a picture in the mind of the desired goal and projects the will toward achieving it. This subtly changes one's energy and awareness, and makes the possibility of obtaining the desired outcome more possible. This is a natural form of magic that is accessible to all, even those without supernatural abilities. This type of focus and direction of energy is generally benign, and although it is possible for anyone to do, it does take time and effort to accomplish, and certainly lacks the spectacle one associates with the practice of magic. In both prayer and magic, patience is essential.

An unintended, and truly magical, aspect of prayer is its timelessness. Prayer happens outside the bounds of time. I have noticed that the effects of prayer can occur much later, or even before prayer. One can perform a Visualization, and find out later that the visualized effect had already been accomplished. The sacred space of prayer takes one to infinite realms.

EREMITICAL LIFE AND PRAYER

Wicca has a long history of solitary practitioners - those who live and practice alone. This is very similar to the Christian hermit tradition, with the notable exception of asceticism. The Christian hermit often lives alone much more strictly and practices more austerity in living than is compatible with Paganism. Wiccan solitaries do not cut themselves off from the rest of society to the same extent; in fact, the solitary aspect of such a life is nearly always confined to ritual practice, which is done alone. Often this is done because witches have no coven available nearby, so must practice alone. What I would like to introduce to Pagans is the notion of intentionally living as a solitary. The intentional choice to do this is what makes a hermit a hermit, rather than simply someone who has come to live alone, perhaps by default. In the case of the solitary Pagan or Wiccan, the practice would be one of simply choosing to live and practice alone, and even spending most of the time alone in order to cultivate a mindful connection to God throughout the day. This does not mean that one has no friends, or never leaves home; it simply means that one chooses to and in fact does spend most of the time alone in meditation or simple mindful awareness of God. I do not see where this would cause any conflict with Wiccan belief and practice, even if there were an available nearby coven.

In fact, having a job outside the home and being married are not incompatible with eremitical life, either (Fredette & Fredette, 2008). Today, it is often impossible to disengage completely from the world, especially during the working years. Income is necessary, and working from home is not always an option. Often the call to solitude comes after marriage, usually in middle age (Fredette & Fredette, 2008). By this time, the devotee may have been married for several years, and if the couple wish to continue their commitment to each other, there is no reason not to. If both partners are amenable, one or both of them can practice an eremitical lifestyle and still continue the marriage. The only life condition I cannot reconcile with eremitism is having children. Children need their parents, and it is extremely unfair to them to engage in such a lifestyle, even if there is another parent or caregiver available. If one is a parent, then the hermit life must wait until the children are grown.

Eremitism is the most extreme form of contemplative prayer, because it is constant prayer. Every activity is devoted to a prayerful awareness of the Divine, and there is a commitment to see the enchantment in everyday things and activities. This is somewhat more involved than the traditional Wiccan solitary life, but not as severe as Christian asceticism. Living this way does not cut one off completely, but does require serious consideration of when and how much to leave one's solitude. To live this way, one must await the coming of the Holy at the thin places between the worlds. Dwelling at the thin places every day takes great strength, and tolerance for unpleasant truths. This is done by engaging in constant prayer, or having an attitude of prayer. Because hermits live at and can see the thin places, they can also point the way to the Holy for others.

One interesting form of eremitical life is the hermit laura, a group of dwellings near each other where hermits live in community. This practice may be more appealing to Pagans than living completely alone, as it involves shared ritual, at least some of the time. This could be accomplished in an urban setting with people living in an apartment building, for example.

At the heart of eremitism is a rejection of the prevailing social values of consumerism and conformity. The real eremitical commitment is to devote oneself to God rather than to fitting in with a mindless materialism, so simply not participating in the expected activities or living by the usual values accomplishes more to separate one than the physical act of living alone. The real contribution here is to stand as a witness against the prevailing social practices and values by not participating. By not buying the latest gadget or attending the most popular event, the hermit or solitary shows that these things are not valued in a life lived in a mindful, spiritual way. Living quietly and thoughtfully with the earth and with God in an intentional way is what makes the life eremitical instead of simply living alone.

This kind of life has its drawbacks. It is never safe to be too different. This type of difference has a prophetic quality; by rejecting the status quo, the hermit shows the uncomfortable and frightening truth of the hollowness of our society, and people do not like this. Often frightened people turn to violence, and those who are too different, such as artists and other creatives, as well as spiritual people, get the brunt of the violence. When one chooses to live an eremitical life, the safe, normal life is left behind.

ENLIGHTENMENT, OR, THE UNITIVE LIFE

The ultimate goal of prayer is to continue it throughout the day, so that it is constant, and all one's moments are lived in awareness of the Divine. Some call it enlightenment; Underhill (1974, p. 413+) calls it the Unitive Life, because union with God has been achieved. The Fredettes (2008, p. 152) suggest that spiritual life must come first, then, all else must be made to follow, including work that is consonant with one's beliefs. When one lives in this manner, and is faithful in one's meditation practice, then that practice gradually moves over into all the activities of daily life. For those who persevere, after much time and effort, a meditative awareness will become the normal state. At this point, as Michaelson (2009, p. 42, 192) suggests, the practitioner realizes that mystical union with God provides the ability to see God everywhere.

It is not necessary, however, to wait for final enlightenment, because it is possible to see God everywhere even if a permanent unitive state has not been achieved. It is sufficient to see the world without the burden of God's full glory, because the glory of God even occasionally and in smaller measure is transformative. In the end, being on the journey is enough, even if it is so long as to take up one's entire life. We then realize that God's sanctified world looks just like everyday life, only enchanted.

CONCLUSION

There are several types of prayer, and all are valid according to need and spiritual level. Ritual is especially good for group worship, as it keeps the congregation focused, and ritual can be used for private prayer as well. The creation of sacred space is a simple and effective ritual that can be used by groups and individuals to bring forward an awareness of the Divine. The prayer style I advocate is simple prayer; listening for and listening to God. The desired result remains the same, regardless of style – a noetic, ineffable experience that is transformative and sustaining. Our experience of God can be immanent or transcendent; what is important is that we experience God and listen.

Magic is generally a seeking after power, which is not compatible with the spirituality I have set forth here. The most magic I advocate is ritual magic, such as the creation of sacred space, or

Visualization. For magic to be safe, it needs to be founded in a firm ethical base, and the practitioner must be very focused, and have an understanding of the broader repercussions of the working. It is simply beyond the scope of most people's vision to see the distant consequences of one's actions, so it is just as well that there are so few people who are capable of magic. Even Visualization must be done with compassion, and the clear intention to do no harm.

Although eremitical life may be too foreign for most Pagans, some may find it intriguing, particularly the hermit laura arrangement, where hermits live in a group. I believe that the eremitical tradition has a great deal to offer Pagans, especially as it is so similar to the Wiccan solitary tradition. Adopting an eremitic lifestyle and spirituality is also the final step in contemplative practice, and those who are contemplative sometimes come to find that becoming more hermit-like is actually comfortable and appealing. Pagans can live a contemplative and even an eremitical life, since the solitude is not strict and no ascetic practices are required. If more Pagans adopted this type of spirituality, the tradition would be enriched.

The goal of prayer is union with God, but this goal takes much time and effort to achieve. It is enough, however, just to work at this goal, because God is also present in the working, not just in the achieving. The enchantment of life is available to all who look for it, not just to the enlightened ones. Ultimately, the best magic is a divine gift, not something we do. The entire world is enchanted; all we have to do is notice. When we take the time to see the enchantment that is everywhere in creation, then we find we do not need magic after all.

Death and the Soul

The immortality of the individual human soul has been part of the Western worldview for many hundreds of years, and lingers to some extent even among those who do not profess any religious belief. Wicca, and Paganism in general, have different views of the soul, what it is, its purpose, and the nature of death. If we adopt the notion of Oneness, we come to conclusions that differ from both the standard Western view as well as traditional Pagan views. Here, we shall explore some of the ramifications of Oneness for our idea of the human soul, and what happens to our souls when we die.

ONENESS

When we consider Oneness and the soul, it becomes apparent that the typical Western notion of soul does not quite apply. If we are all One, if we participate in divinity and God is everywhere, do we have individual souls? If we have individual souls, what happens to them after death? Certainly there is no doctrine of salvation among Pagans, such as Christians have, as we do not consider ourselves in need of it. What is the purpose of a soul, then? What is a soul?

Our souls are those divine parts of us that participate in God, and that we consider ours while we live in our bodies. After death, our souls merge into the One again. That soul that endures and returns to the One is God, living in each person, allowing us to participate in divinity. A soul is simply a piece of divinity; it is our

CHAPTER SIX: DEATH AND THE SOUL

own spark of God's life that makes us One with God, each other, and the universe. As far as I can see, we do not have eternal individual souls that are distinct from other souls.

There are many Pagans who consider the soul to be multiple, often threefold (Kraemer, 2012). In one system, for example, it is believed that one soul is the animal soul which animates the body, another is the human soul which provides intelligence and personality and the distinctively human attributes of a person, and the third, is the divine soul. The only one I consider a soul is this third soul, the divine essence in each person that joins us to God, and that returns to God upon our death. The animal soul I see as really only the chemical energy that powers our bodies, and the human soul is the result of genetics and environment that gives us our personalities and intelligence and our distinctive way in the world. To me, the soul is exclusively divine; anything else is chemical or biological energy. Although all natural processes are part of God's life in the world, they are not God, while our souls are. They are our own sparks of divinity that make us One with God and all of creation.

DEATH

If we consider salvation irrelevant, what is the purpose of a soul? Our souls are God's life within us, joining us to God while we live. After death, our bodies return to being an assemblage of chemicals and microorganisms, and our souls merge into the One again. This could be considered a sort of reincarnation, a reincarnation that is the recycling of our chemical energy, and the return of our souls to the One. It seems to me, that each individual is who they are based on their biology rather than their soul, with our personality and intelligence and all the rest of us being the expression of our physiology and genetics, and when we die, it is gone. Since we are products of not only our genetics, but also of our environments, any individual is a completely new person, not someone from another lifetime reborn to a new era. Time has moved on, and the unique genetic and environmental components that produced a deceased individual are gone. The soul that endures and returns to the One is God, living in each person and allowing them to participate in divinity. Our bodies provide our individuality while our souls join us to everyone and everything else, giving us our unity, our expression of Oneness in creation.

Because our souls join us to God and the universe, reincarnation could also be seen as a carrying forward of divine energy in order to promote the progress of humanity. In this way, reincarnation is not the reincarnation of one soul, but the moving forward of purpose over time. People have always sought to live in better ways and have developed new technology to help them do work and make life safer and more enjoyable. Recently, people also have begun to improve society by fostering social justice and human welfare through both government and private programs. Both technological and social progress occurs in small increments over generations, so no one person can carry these changes forward. Rather, in each generation, a new person takes up the standard and helps move things forward, reincarnating purpose rather than person.

The case can be made that we do not have individual souls as such, since they do not endure individually after death. If our souls simply merge with the One upon death, and do not provide our individuality or our salvation, then perhaps they are not personal, individual souls that are unique to us. But does that matter? The primary benefit is participation in God's life, which is such a blessing that it renders the other concerns much less significant. I find it an inestimable privilege to participate in God's divinity, even if only for my individual lifespan.

THE DIVINITY OF THINGS

Do animals or objects have souls? I believe all things participate in divinity, because they are part of creation, and so are One with God. Even manufactured objects such as automobiles participate in divinity because all the materials used to make them come from the natural world. Objects such as rocks that have little or no self-determination participate in divinity, but do they have souls? Perhaps the real question here is, are objects persons?

Some have been concerned that robots may enjoy personhood, or even the possession of a soul, especially if they have self-awareness and self-determination. Regardless of ability, a robot is a machine, and can only do what it is made to do. A robot can be made to move around, communicate, and perform tasks like a human would, but it is still a machine. Even if a robot has an ethics program, the decisions it would make would be a result of its programming, and not of its own independent consideration. Although such a robot might have a level of "free will" similar to ours (please see Chapter Four), that still cannot imply personhood. Some may equate human genetics with a robot's programming, but I firmly disagree. An engineer wrote the programming code, but God wrote the genetic code. For me, this is what distinguishes artificial intelligence (AI) from a human; the human is a natural individual, and their decisions have moral weight. Since none of the ethical decisions made by an AI entity would be natural decisions, made by a natural individual, they would have no ethical weight, because the responsibility for its behavior would fall ultimately on its maker rather than on the robot itself. The bestowal of self-awareness or an ethics program on a machine by its maker simply does not bring with it personhood or a soul. The AI entity would participate in divinity no more and no less than any other nonliving object.

Objects of any kind are not persons. Personhood belongs primarily to humans, and to a lesser extent to animals as well, as they usually lack self-awareness and ethical weight, and sometimes even self-determination. Sometimes, though, it seems that animals are closer to God than we are, for all our vaunted self-awareness. Since animals usually lack self-awareness, it may be that they are not aware of God either, or perhaps they are as aware of God as a fish is aware of the water it swims in. But do they have souls?

Animals, too, have their own souls, a share in divinity that many of us recognize. Animals deserve honor and consideration, just as we do. The personality and self-determination present in animals is not due to their souls, but to their physiology, just as ours is. It enables us to recognize the presence of a self and relate to it, even though that self is often not self-aware, but it is their souls that call for our respect.

This applies to all animals – wild animals, pets, and livestock that are used for food. Animals should not be abused, which brings into question their use as pets and food, even their use for work. The use of animals for food is the most difficult issue, and many Pagans are, laudably, vegetarian. Still, animals provide a superb source of dietary protein, and our ancestors ate meat whenever they could. This long-standing practice and its nutritional value must be acknowledged, but a better way of life for domestic animals should also be devised. I have long shrunk from taking an animal as a pet, since I consider it disrespectful to them because they are perfectly capable of having satisfying lives without us. I find it far more rewarding to befriend or just commune with a wild animal than enjoy the forced friendship of a pet who had no choice.

As stated previously, Animism is a common belief among Pagans, and involves worshipping spirits of trees, mountains, springs, and so forth. Animists conduct devotional practices to honor favored spirits, and this reflects a certain amount of truth, as all things participate in divinity. However, even though everything participates in divinity, only God is fully God, and the worship of objects or places or any other finite thing seems almost meaningless, as the divinity it shares is not too much different from any other object or place, or even one's own. According to this notion, should we not honor all things and persons? This seems a much better foundation for ethical behavior and sound environmental stewardship than for worship. This is not to say that well-dressing or honoring a sacred tree should not be done, but that it should be done recognizing that God is present in the tree, not that the tree is a god.

CONCLUSION

So, do we all have souls - animals, people, and things? God is present in all things, but maybe that is not the same as having a soul. Since we do not need our souls to convey salvation or provide a personality, maybe we do not have souls after all. However, I do firmly believe that God is in each of us, although perhaps in different measures. God is present in a rock, but in a different degree or way than It is present in you. Holiness is everywhere, and it is impossible for us to say exactly how much is present where or in different creatures. For now, I am content to count that as both a mystery and a blessing, and attempt to revere all of creation.

Conclusion

Oneness and contemplative practice are Contemplative Wicca's most salutary attributes, and also provide its distinctive differences from traditional Wicca, but because Contemplative Wicca is based in the sacredness of nature, it follows the Wiccan path regardless of its differences with tradition. Along with this, the belief in the sacredness of nature provides the foundation for a system of spiritual practice and ethics that allows us to see the unity of creation and each other, and moves us forward to a more harmonious society.

Sharing our practice with others in interfaith exchanges can help to lead society to new ideas and ways of living that provide greater benefit than we are experiencing now from the religions that have held sway for so long. It may be, however, that many Pagans are still too new in Paganism, and that it is difficult for them yet to reach out in interfaith contexts with tolerance for different traditions, particularly the Abrahamic traditions. Many Pagans continue to struggle to clarify who they are, and remain focused on themselves. Theology is the essential work that will help us to consolidate our identity and move forward as a faith tradition among other faith traditions. The fruit of this theological work is charitable service to the larger community, which is not yet a prominent feature of many Pagan groups. Only when we are more certain of who we are, can we share with others, with mutual benefit. It is important for Wiccans to practice theological thought and discourse not only to clearly form our own thinking, but also to guide our lives. Pagan ethics especially could benefit from the support of a firm theology based on Oneness, with cautiously selective adoption of older values and modes of thought. The values that have arisen through theological reflection on contemplative experience need to be articulated so we may form a more complete and coherent Pagan theology that will guide our lives and reshape society for a new world. When we have done this, we can reach out to others in service, and it is service that will show others that we are serious about our faith, and that our faith is genuine.

Even when we have clarified our beliefs, we should not stand rigidly upon any one system of belief or hold too tightly to dogma. Oneness is not the same as conformity. Rather, we should all share our version of Divine Truth and take joy in our variety, knowing we are all traveling toward the same goal, albeit by different roads. Even though we do not all share the same beliefs, we could and should come together to share in doing the right things. Regardless of belief, we can meditate, celebrate, and serve each other and the world, together.

Humanity's ancient gods do not help us address our current situation. Progress is necessary, as well as desirable, and to further it we must develop an integrated understanding that includes science and religion, accept multiple spiritual viewpoints, and remember that our notions of God are only partial anyway. What we need now is a new, all-embracing idea of God that allows us to avoid tribalism and a small worldview. God is simply God, the creator and sustainer of all that is. We must not attribute to God anthropomorphic notions that are only limiting and divisive.

Psychology provides little assistance in understanding spirituality, and studies reach varying and even conflicting conclusions because there are no agreed-upon definitions to guide research in the psychology of religion. The exception is developmental psychology, which is more helpful than not in illuminating how we grow morally and spiritually. Additionally, some studies have shown that meditation promotes spiritual and physical well-being, and enlarges the practitioner's awareness and sphere of moral concern. Other than this, it seems we must rely on traditional teachings and methods, and heed the call of the Divine to learn our path in life.

The God Who inspires and Who is found in contemplative prayer is not only transcendent, but also immanent; God is everywhere and all creation participates in divine life. This view of God inspires collaboration and sharing, rather than oppression and aggression, and our way of life must reflect this. God is the ground of being, creates and sustains everything, and is One. We have sufficient independence to see that God is not only immanent but transcendent, and this inspires our awe. God is also the union of opposites, including even those things we consider evil, and the contemplative path allows us to differentiate evil from good, and to begin to reconcile and embrace the paradox of divinity. God is everywhere and everything is holy. It is this notion of God that is the defining characteristic of this theology and from which all else must flow.

There are many obstacles to promoting a contemplative Pagan theology of Oneness. Contemplatives are subject to societal and scientific misunderstanding. Society considers contemplatives suspect, or at least irrelevant. There is no support in mainstream society for contemplative life, because society values speed and superficiality rather than patience and depth of understanding. Those who seek a contemplative life must have the strength to go forth alone and accept that conventional society will not appreciate them or their efforts.

A contemplative Pagan theology of Oneness has an important contribution to make nevertheless. When our belief in Oneness guides our behavior and thinking, we can remake the world into a happier, more just place where we help people make a contribution to society rather than simply establish guilt and mete out punishment to those who do not conform. By refusing to accept mindless conformity, we provide a beacon of light to lead society forward. By resisting crass materialism we show that there is a better way to live that includes all, not just the rich and powerful, and that what is most important is not material prosperity, but our participation in Divinity.

We are all different, and have different truths. What works spiritually for one person may not work for another. There are very few absolutes, and there are usually several good alternatives to the "one way" to do anything. Though there are many valid ways to pray, the goal remains the same – union with the Divine. We are all leaves of the tree of life, and even though each one of us is different, we are all connected to the tree. We are united because we have all come from the same place, and are rooted in the same place, and this fundamental unity must be honored.

Our purpose in life is to live rightly. To do this, we need both science and religion. Learning and understanding are necessary spiritually as well as practically. It is necessary to know what things are and how they work, but that is not enough. Science tells us what, how, and when, but religion tells us why. Humans have always wondered why, and indeed, why is the best question. Religion helps us discover the meanings of things, and allows us to discern our purpose. The two types of knowing are incomplete without each other. When we have achieved congruence between science and spirit, perhaps then we shall have achieved wisdom.

When we live rightly, all of our activities are praise, and not just specific religious acts done in a temple. All of the work we do is praise, and so is our tapestry of beliefs, which show us how to live rightly. Learning and teaching are especially praiseful activities because they help ensure that knowledge is preserved and passed on so that future generations can continue to live rightly. (Le Guin, 2000.)

Here, I have attempted to show how Oneness can be applied to Wicca to create a coherent and life-giving contemplative spirituality. Oneness is a unifying force that allows us to not only accept our diversity, but rejoice in it, and lead us into a better future. A natural extension of the Wiccan solitary tradition is an exclusively contemplative practice, which would be enriching both for society and for Paganism. This enrichment can reveal to us the real magic of the world, and allow us to see the enchantment that is present everywhere and in everything.

References

Adler, M. (1986). *Drawing Down the Moon*. Boston: Beacon Press.

Argyle, M., & Hills, P. (2000). Religious experiences and their relations with happiness and personality. *International Journal for the Psychology of Religion, 10*: 157–172.

Aron, E. N. (1996). *The Highly Sensitive Person*. New York: Broadway Books.

Aron, E. N., & Aron, A. (1997). Sensory-processing sensitivity and its relation to introversion and emotionality. *Journal of Personality and Social Psychology, 73*: 345-368.

Barrett, C. E., & Roesch, S. C. (2009). Evaluating the relationship between the five-factor model of personality and religious orientation. *Journal of Psychology and Christianity, 28*: 195-199.

Batson, C. D., Schoenrade, P., & Ventis, W. L. (1993). *Religion and the Individual: a Social-Psychological Perspective*. NY: Oxford University Press.

Bonewits, P. E. I. (1989). *Real Magic*. York Beach ME: Samuel Weiser.

Carpenter, D. D. Spiritual Contours of the Contemporary Pagan Worldview. Online article downloaded 8/27/14, https://www.circlesanctuary.org/index.php/about-paganism/spiritual-contours-of-the-contemporary-pagan-worldview.

Casey, J. (1990). *Pagan Virtue: an Essay in Ethics*. Oxford, UK: Clarendon Press.

Chandler, H. M., Alexander, C. N., & Heaton, D. P. (2005). The transcendental meditation program and postconventional self-development: A 10-year longitudinal study. *Journal of Social Behavior and Personality, 17*: 93-121.

Christ, C. P. (1997). *Rebirth of the Goddess: Finding Meaning in Feminist Spirituality*. Reading MA: Addison-Wesley.

Chupp, T. (1985). Disaffected Roman Catholics: Developmental considerations. *Pastoral Psychology, 34*: 92-100.

Clark, N. (2015). Stephen Hawking: Aggression could destroy us. *The Independent*, 2/19/15, http://www.independent.co.uk/news/science/stephen-hawking-aggression-could-destroy-us-10057658.html

Cook, C. C. H. (2004). Psychiatry and mysticism. *Mental Health, Religion and Culture, 7*: 149–163.

Cooper, J. W. (2006). *Panentheism: the Other God of the Philosophers*. Grand Rapids, MI: Baker Academic.

d'Aquili, E., & Newberg, A. B. (1999). *The Mystical Mind: Probing the Biology of Religious Experience*. Minneapolis: Fortress Press.

Derezotes, D. (2000). Evaluation of yoga and meditation trainings with adolescent sex offenders. *Child and Adolescent Social Work Journal, 17*: 98-113.

Einolf, C. J. (2013). Daily spiritual experiences and prosocial behavior. *Social Indicators Research, 110*: 71-87.

Flere, S., & Lavrič, M. (2008). Is intrinsic religious orientation a culturally specific American Protestant concept? The fusion of intrinsic and extrinsic religious orientation among non-Protestants. *European Journal of Social Psychology, 38*: 521–530.

Forbes, D. (2003). Turn the wheel: integral school counseling for male adolescents. *Journal of Counseling and Development*, 81: 142-149.

Fowler, J. W. (1981). *Stages of Faith*. San Francisco: Harper and Row.

Francis, L. J. (2007). Introducing the new indices of religious orientation (NIRO): conceptualization and measurement. *Mental Health, Religion and Culture, 10*: 585-602.

Francis, L. J. (2010). Personality and religious orientation: Shifting sands or firm foundations? *Mental Health, Religion and Culture, 13*: 793–803.

Francis, L. J., Jewell, A., & Robbins, M. (2010). The relationship between religious orientation, personality, and purpose in life among an older Methodist sample. *Mental Health, Religion and Culture, 13*: 777-791.

Francis, L. J., Robbins, M., & Murray, L. (2010). Psychological type and religious orientation: Do introverts and extraverts go to church for different reasons? *Mental Health, Religion and Culture, 13*: 821-827.

Fredette, P. A., & Fredette, K. K. (2008). *Consider the Ravens*. Bloomington IN: iUniverse.

Garfield, A. M., Kortenkamp, K. V., Drwecki, B. B., Gracz, M. D., & Moore, C. F. (2014). The oneness beliefs scale: connecting spirituality with pro-environmental behavior. *Journal for the Scientific Study of Religion, 53*: 356-372.

Gross, R. M. (1999). Religious diversity: some implications for monotheism. *Cross Currents, 49*: 349-366.

Harrison, V. S. (1999). Personal identity and integration: Von Balthasar's phenomenology of human holiness. *Heythrop Journal, 40*: 424-437.

Harrow, J. (1996). The contemporary Neo-pagan revival. In: J. R. Lewis (Ed.), *Magical Religion and Modern Witchcraft* (pp. 9-24). Albany, NY: SUNY Press, 1996.

Holm, N. G. (1982). Mysticism and intense experiences. *Journal for the Scientific Study of Religion, 21*: 268–277.

Hood, Jr., R. W., Ghorbani, N., Watson, P. J., Ghramaleki, A. F., Bing, M. N., Davison, H. K., Morris, R. J., & Williamson, W. P. (2001). Dimensions of the mysticism scale: confirming the three-factor structure in the United States and Iran. *Journal for the Scientific Study of Religion, 40*: 691–705.

Hood, Jr., R. W., Hill, P. C., & Spilka, B. (2009). *The Psychology of Religion: an Empirical Approach* (4th edn). New York: Guilford Press.

Istrate, E., & Knudsen, B. (2016, January). *County Economies 2015: Opportunities and Challenges* (NACo Trends Analysis Paper Series No. 5). Washington, D.C.: National Association of Counties. http://www.naco.org/resources/county-economies-opportunities-challenges

James, W. (1958). *The Varieties of Religious Experience*. New York: New American Library.

Ji, C. C. (2004). Religious orientations in moral development. *Journal of Psychology and Christianity*, 23: 22-30.

Jones, R. P., Cox, D., Cooper, B., & Lienesch, R. (2015). *Anxiety, Nostalgia and Mistrust*: Findings from the 2015 American Values Survey. Washington, D.C.: Public Religion Research Institute. http://publicreligion.org/site/wp-content/uploads/2015/11/PRRI-AVS-2015.pdf

Kaldor, P., Francis, L. J., & Fisher, J. W. (2002). Personality and spirituality: Christian prayer and eastern meditation are not the same. *Pastoral Psychology, 50*: 165–172.

Kaleem, J. (2015). Reading, writing, required silence: how meditation is changing schools and students. *The Huffington Post*, 6/12/15. http://www.huffingtonpost.com/2015/06/12/schools-meditation-quiet-time_n_7544582.html

Kraemer, C. H. (2012). *Seeking the Mystery: an Introduction to Pagan Theologies*. Englewood, CO: Patheos Press.

Kroll, J., Bachrach, B., & Carey K. (2002). A reappraisal of medieval mysticism and hysteria. *Mental Health, Religion and Culture, 5*: 83-98.

La Forge, P. G. (2000). Four steps to a fundamental ethical vision through meditation. *Journal of Business Ethics, 28*: 25-34.

Le Guin, U. K. (2000). *The Telling*. New York: Harcourt.

Mantin, R. (2004). Thealogies in process: re-searching and theorizing spiritualities, subjectivities, and Goddess-talk. In: J. Blain, D. Ezzy, G. Harvey (Eds.), *Researching Paganisms* (147-169). Walnut Creek, CA: Alta Mira Press.

Maxwell, T. P. (2003). Integral spirituality, deep science, and ecological awareness. *Zygon: Journal of Religion and Science, 38*: 257-276.

McFague, S. (1982). *Metaphorical Theology*. Philadelphia, PA: Fortress Press.

McNamara, P. (2002). The motivational origins of religious practices. *Zygon: Journal of Religion and Science, 37*: 143-161.

McRae, E. (2013). Equanimity and intimacy: a Buddhist-feminist approach to the elimination of bias. *Sophia International Journal of Philosophy and Traditions, 52*: 447-462.

Michaelson, J. (2009). *Everything is God: the Radical Path of Nondual Judaism*. Boston: Trumpeter.

Michalon, M. (2001). "Selflessness" in the service of the ego: contributions, limitations and dangers of Buddhist psychology for Western psychology. *American Journal of Psychotherapy, 55*: 202-19.

Neyrinck, B., Lens, W., Vansteenkiste, M., & Soenens, B. (2010). Updating Allport's and Batson's framework of religious orientations: a reevaluation from the perspective of self-determination theory and Wulff's social cognitive model. *Journal for the Scientific Study of Religion, 49*: 425-438.

Nidich, S. I., Nidich, R. J., & Alexander, C. N. (2000). Moral development and higher states of consciousness. *Journal of Adult Development, 7*: 217-225.

Nidich, S. I., Schneider, R. H., Nidich, R. J., Foster, G., Sharma, H., Salerno, J., Goodman, R., & Alexander, C. N. (2005). Effect of the transcendental meditation program on intellectual development in community-dwelling older adults. *Journal of Social Behavior and Personality, 17*: 217–226.

Noble, K. G., Houston, S. M., Brito, N. H., Bartsch, H., Kan, E., Kuperman, J. M., Akshoomoff, N., Amaral, D. G., Bloss, C. S., Libiger, O., Schork, N. J., Murray, S. S., Casey, B. J., Chang, L., Ernst, T. M., Frazier, J. A., Gruen, J. R., Kennedy, D. N., Van Zijl, P., Mostofsky, S., Kaufmann, W. E., Kenet, T., Dale, A. M., Jernigan, T. L., & Sowell, E. R. (2015). Family income, parental education and brain structure in children and adolescents. *Nature Neuroscience, 18*: 773–778.

O'Connor, M. (2002). Spiritual dark night and psychological depression: some comparisons and considerations. *Counseling and Values, 46*: 137-149.

Peterson, E. H. (2003). Transparent lives: the contemplative Christian. *Christian Century, 120*:24, 20-27.

Plank, K. A. (2002). Thomas Merton and the ethical edge of contemplation. *Anglican Theological Review, 84*: 113-126.

Robbins, M., Francis, L., McIlroy, D., Clarke, R., & Pritchard, L. (2010). Three religious orientations and five personality factors: An exploratory study among adults in England. *Mental Health, Religion and Culture, 13*: 771-775.

Ross, C. F. J., & Francis, L. J. (2010). The relationship of intrinsic, extrinsic, and quest religious orientations to Jungian psychological type among churchgoers in England and Wales. *Mental Health, Religion and Culture, 13:* 805-819.

Saucier, G., & Skrzypińska, K. (2006). Spiritual but not religious? evidence for two independent dispositions. *Journal of Personality, 74*: 1257-1292.

Schwenka, S. (2000). Mysticism as a predictor of subjective well-being. *International Journal for the Psychology of Religion, 10*: 259–269.

Spanos, N. P., & Moretti, P. (1988). Correlates of mystical and diabolical experiences in a sample of female university students. *Journal for the Scientific Study of Religion, 27*: 105 – 116.

Spilka, B., & Schmidt, G. (1983). General attribution theory for the psychology of religion: the influence of event-character on attributions to God. *Journal for the Scientific Study of Religion, 22*: 326-339.

Stifler, K., Greer, J., Sneck, W., & Dovenmuehle, R. (1993). An empirical investigation of the discriminability of reported mystical experiences among religious contemplatives, psychotic inpatients, and normal adults. *Journal for the Scientific Study of Religion, 32*: 366–372.

Tang, Y., Lu, Q., Geng, X., Elliot A., Stein, E. A., Yang, Y., & Posner, M. I. (2010). Short-term meditation induces white matter changes in the anterior cingulate. *Proceedings of the National Academy of Sciences, 107*: 15649–15652.

Taylor, B. (2010). *Dark Green Religion*. Berkeley: University of California Press.

Underhill, E. (1974). *Mysticism*. New York: New American Library.

Werblowsky, R. J. Z. (1985). What's in a name: Reflections on god, gods and the divine. *Japanese Journal of Religious Studies, 12*: 3-16.

Wikstrom, O. (1987). Attribution, roles and religion: A theoretical analysis of Sunden's role theory of religion and the attributional approach to religious experience. *Journal for the Scientific Study of Religion, 26*: 390-400.

Wilson, T. D., Reinhard, D. A., Westgate, E. C., Gilbert, D. T., Ellerbeck, N., Hahn, C., Brown, C. L., & Shaked, A. (2014). Just think: The challenges of the disengaged mind. *Science, 345*: 6192, 75-77.

Winterowd, C., Harrist, S., Thomason, N., Worth, S., & Carlozzi, B. (2005). The relationship of spiritual beliefs and involvement with the experience of anger and stress in college students. *Journal of College Student Development, 46*: 515-529.

Wong-McDonald, A., & Gorsuch, R. L. (2004). A multivariate theory of God concept, religious motivation, locus of control, coping, and spiritual well-being. *Journal of Psychology and Theology, 32*: 318–334.

Wright, D. S. (2006). *Satori* and the moral dimension of enlightenment. *Journal of Buddhist Ethics, 13*.

York, M. (2003). *Pagan Theology*. NY: New York University Press.

Index